Zha Methodology for Sustainability Mindset - Sustainability Practitioners Certifications

"Scaling the maturity of the practitioners"

Volume - 2

Author Karki Ashokkumar

Made with ❤ on the Notion Press Platform

www.notionpress.co

Thank you to all the Zha Foundation advisory board members, all highly esteemed members of the board and club, for your great support and encouragement in doing greater innovative social work in the concept of sustainable development.

Dear Ms. Prasanna Devi and Mr. Abineshwaran Elangovan,

We are writing this letter to extend my heartfelt gratitude for your invaluable support in researching the ZHA Sustainability Mindset Curriculum Club Activities. Your collective insights and diverse perspectives have been instrumental in deepening our understanding and advancing our work.

Thank you once again for your unwavering support and commitment.

Warm regards,

Karki Ashokkumar	Parimala Ashokkumar	M Sabarinathan
Founder and Mentor,	President & Treasurer	Vice President,
ZHA Foundation	ZHA Foundation	ZHA Foundation
Charitable Trust,	Charitable Trust,	Charitable Trust,
Tamil Nadu, India	Tamil Nadu, India	Tamil Nadu, India

Rationale: A Tribute to the Seeds of a Sustainability Mindset

The Zha foundation of the Zha Methodology for Sustainability Mindset is deeply personal. It was not conceived in a laboratory or business think tank, but rather, born from a quiet revolution in the heart of a young boy in Madurai. That boy Karki Ashokkumar, now an senior executive technology leader and sustainability practitioner was unknowingly shaped by one of his earliest mentors, Mrs. Premalatha Paneerselvam, the founder of Mahatma Schools in Madurai.

During (1991-1995) his 6th to 10th standard, Karki was a student at Mahatma School, where weekends were not just days of rest but of learning beyond classrooms. Under the visionary guidance of   Mrs. Premalatha, students especially hostelites and non hostelites volunteers, were taken to nearby villages to engage in community exposure activities. What seemed like simple weekend initiatives later revealed themselves as profound value instillation exercises.

Mrs. Premalatha Paneerselvam was far ahead of her time. She championed a form of education that emphasized value based development over commercial success, and purposeful living over material accumulation. Her approach naturally embedded the spirit of sustainability long before the term became a global mandate. She encouraged students to observe and serve the rural underprivileged, to see dignity in simplicity, and to understand how real transformation begins with empathy and selflessness.

Although she never labeled her method as "sustainability education," her lived values planted the earliest seeds of a sustainability mindset in young Karki. This silent yet powerful pedagogy became the reference point of reflection in his adult life, especially as he grew increasingly disturbed by the widespread greed-driven mindset he witnessed in the corporate and agricultural sectors. Decisions made without regard for people, the planet, or the long-term good were causing irreparable damage.

In his journey of self-realization, Mr. Karki traced back his sense of "feeling sufficient" and his innate desire to enable others not dominate as qualities directly shaped by Mrs. Premalatha's early influence. Her undocumented, intuitive approach to nurturing students with empathy, kindness, social responsibility, and exposure to sustainable living was a legacy that deserved formal acknowledgment.

This chapter, therefore, is not just a tribute but a rationale. A rationale for why sustainability must be taught as a mindset, not just a policy. It is a conscious effort to give structure and visibility to a philosophy that once shaped a few but now has the power to shape many.

Through this chapter, Mr. Karki honors the silent educators like Mrs. Premalatha who raised generations of sustainability-minded citizens not by preaching, but by exposing young hearts to real-world needs and allowing them to feel purpose through service. This ideology is now being systematized by Mr. Karki into the Zha Methodology for Sustainability Mindset, expressed through four levels of maturity and twelve certifications a structured path to scale the development of sustainability consciousness across the globe.

In essence, the Rationale marks the origin story of the methodology. Our intention for serving the world of young generation to adapt this co-curriculum such that every great schooling begins with a small seed and this seed was compassion, planted in the fertile minds of children, by a woman who believed that real education is the one that makes us more conscious responsible humans.

This belief led the Zha Foundation to explore a joint venture with Mahatma Schools in Madurai, in piloting the concept of sustainability mindset research and later provide the concept to others schools through a unique eco club co-curriculum ways of activities. In 2024, we piloted the Sustainability Mindset Curriculum in three institutions: Mahatma Gateway School in Madurai, Corporation Schools in Coimbatore, and Muvendar Matriculation Higher Secondary School in Peravurani, Thanjavur District. The results were promising: parents witnessed a remarkable shift in their children's choices, with hobbies and interests increasingly focused on nature, animals, and overall well-being.

Preface:

Zha Foundations' Founder Mr. Karki Ashokkumar gained valuable global perspectives through his experiences living in countries like Canada and the United States. These environments, with their progressive approaches to nature and sustainability, stood in stark contrast to the prevailing attitudes he observed in India. He noticed that while sustainability policies were being advocated by the Indian government, there was a lack of understanding and commitment among the general population. The gap, particularly influenced by greed and selfishness, continued even in the era of technological advancement.

Need for Sustainability Mindset:

Recognizing the importance of addressing this gap, Karki Ashokkumar envisioned a framework for sustainability mindset enabling people to embrace sustainable practices. He understood that merely having policies in place was not sufficient; there was a need to educate and empower individuals to make sustainable choices in their daily lives. ZHA fostering Sustainability Mindset for People reinstates that change starts from you.

Our Sustainability Priorities

Global Professional Community Engagement:

To leverage expertise and perspectives from around the world, Karki Ashokkumar sought the involvement of the global professional community in leading the initiative. By inviting professionals from diverse backgrounds to become advisory members of the **Zha Sustainability Practitioners Club (ZSPC),** he aimed to foster collaboration and knowledge sharing on sustainable practices.

ZHA Foundation Ethics:

Drawing from his upbringing in the villages and suburbs of Tamil Nadu, India, Karki Ashokkumar emphasized the importance of social responsibility, commitment, courage, openness and integrity as foundational ethics. He recognized the need to combat the prevalent mindset of greed and selfishness by promoting values that prioritize the well-being of society and the environment.

Examples:

1. *Cross-Cultural Observations:* Karki Ashokkumar's experiences living in different countries allowed him to observe varying attitudes towards sustainability and environmental stewardship. For instance, he noticed a stronger culture of recycling and conservation in Canada compared to India.

2. *Government Policies vs. Public Understanding:* Despite the Indian government's efforts to promote sustainability policies, Karki Ashokkumar observed a disconnect between policy implementation and public understanding. For example, while regulations might be in place to reduce plastic waste, public awareness and compliance could be lacking.

3. *Global Professional Community Engagement:* Karki Ashokkumar's invitation for professionals from around the world to join the ZSPC as advisory members demonstrates his commitment to leveraging diverse expertise. For instance, professionals from the US might bring insights on sustainable business practices, while those from Canada might offer perspectives on environmental conservation.

4. *Foundation Ethics in Action:* Karki Ashokkumar's emphasis on social equality and responsibility can be reflected in initiatives undertaken by the Zha Foundation Charitable Trust. For example, the trust might prioritize projects that benefit marginalized communities or promote sustainable livelihoods in rural areas.

TABLE OF CONTENTS

PROGRESSION OVERVIEW

Basic (Level 1): Awareness and foundational skills.

Intermediate (Level 2): Sustainable systems thinking and problem solving.

Advanced (Level 3): Leadership in Sustainability and Global perspectives.

Expert (Level 4): Specialized Skill and Policy Advocacy in Sustainability.

CHAPTERS & CERTIFICATIONS

This structured framework ensures a progressive and comprehensive approach to sustainability education and leadership.

Background

How Small Human Actions Make a Big Impact

Individual actions, though seemingly minor, can collectively lead to significant environmental and social changes. Simple habits like reducing energy consumption, recycling, conserving water, and supporting local businesses contribute to larger sustainability goals. When adopted by many, these actions can lead to reduced pollution, conservation of resources, and strengthened communities.

Real-Life Stories of Young Sustainability Champions

- **Greta Thunberg**: Starting with solitary climate strikes, Greta inspired a global movement among youth to demand action against climate change.
- **Boyan Slat**: At 18, Boyan founded The Ocean Cleanup, developing innovative solutions to remove plastic from oceans.
- **Autumn Peltier**: A young advocate for clean water, Autumn has addressed international forums, emphasizing the importance of water conservation and indigenous rights.

These examples illustrate how young individuals can drive significant change through passion and commitment.

To scale sustainability mindset practitioners' maturity, we need a structured approach that transitions individuals from self-centered, short-term thinking (rooted in destructive behaviors and greed-driven decisions) to global responsibility, ethical leadership, and long-term sustainable innovation. The ZHA Sustainability Mindset Practitioners Framework provides a strategic roadmap to achieve this transformation and prepare future leaders, entrepreneurs, and corporate professionals for a sustainable future.

The Core Problem: Overcoming Destructive or Irresponsible Human Mindsets

Humanity faces a crisis of short-sighted, profit-driven decisions, leading to:

- Environmental Destruction – Overexploitation of resources, deforestation, biodiversity loss
- Greedy Decision-Making – Corporate exploitation, unsustainable supply chains, consumerism
- Social Inequality – Unequal access to resources, wealth concentration, lack of sustainability education
- Technological Myopia – Innovation driven by profit rather than ethics and long-term sustainability
- To counter these destructive behaviors, individuals need to evolve from reactive, self-serving mindsets to proactive, sustainability-driven leadership.

The ZHA Sustainability Mindset Practitioners Framework: A Structured Maturity Model

This four-tier maturity model ensures a progressive shift from awareness to leadership in sustainability:

Level 1: Awareness & Foundational Skills (Basic) – Practitioners Thinking Maturity

Goal: Break habitual destructive behaviors by embedding sustainability principles.

- Understand Sustainability Mindset Values (White HAT Certification)
- Learn about ecosystem preservation, waste management, and biodiversity conservation
- Real-world actions: Community cleanups, recycling programs, and social equity projects

Mindset Shift: From "I am just one person" to "My actions have a direct impact."

Level 2: Systems Thinking & Problem Solving (Intermediate) – Global Responsibility Maturity

Goal: Expand thinking to recognize sustainability as a systemic issue requiring collective action.

- Apply circular economy models, sustainable agriculture, and energy efficiency strategies
- Engage in policy advocacy, carbon footprint reduction, and leadership for change
- Real-world actions: Organizing sustainability campaigns, networking for impact, promoting ethical consumerism

Mindset Shift: From "Sustainability is just about the environment" to "It's about economic, social, and technological systems."

Level 3: Leadership & Global Perspectives (Advanced) – Future Leaders Maturity

Goal: Develop visionary sustainability leaders who can transform industries and policy.

- Ethical leadership (Pink HAT), global sustainability policies, and climate resilience strategies
- Deep dive into ESG (Environmental, Social, Governance) and corporate sustainability innovation
- Real-world actions: Leading industry collaborations, designing sustainability impact strategies, tackling deforestation, and crisis management

Mindset Shift: From "Sustainability is about reducing harm" to "Sustainability is a driver of innovation and social impact."

Level 4: Specialized Skills & Policy Advocacy (Expert) – Global Changemakers Maturity
Goal: Train entrepreneurs, corporate leaders, and policymakers to drive large-scale sustainability solutions.

- Master advanced ESG compliance, green finance, precision farming, and AI-powered sustainability
- Implement sustainable supply chains, carbon-neutral technologies, and international trade policies
- Real-world actions: Establishing global sustainability communities, corporate ESG implementation, developing smart cities and AI-driven conservation

Mindset Shift: From "Sustainability is an industry responsibility" to "Sustainability is a competitive advantage and a moral obligation."

Scaling Impact: How to Grow Sustainability Mindset Practitioners Globally

1. Gamified Learning & Certification Pathways – Encourage participation through achievements, badges, and recognition (aligned with ZHA Hat Certifications).

2. Club Model to Mentor through Social Activities, Conferences & Industry Partnerships – Connect practitioners with Thought leaders, sustainability experts, and global networks.

3. Real-World Implementation Projects – Ensure hands-on experience via impact-driven sustainability challenges.

4. Tech-Enabled Knowledge Sharing – Use AI-driven platforms, sustainability apps, and blockchain-backed certification tracking for scalability.

5. Policy Advocacy & CSR Collaborations – Work with governments, corporations, and educational institutions to implement sustainability mindset training at a national and global level.

Final Outcome: A New Generation of Global Sustainability Leaders

By following this structured ZHA Sustainability Mindset Maturity Framework, we can transform mindsets, scale sustainability leadership globally, and prepare future tech and corporate innovators who prioritize long-term global responsibility over short-term gains.

CHAPTER 1

Zha White Hat Certification

(Basic - Level 1) - Sustainability Mindset Values, Ecosystem, Waste Management, and Biodiversity

Why Do We Need a Sustainability Mindset?
A sustainability mindset is essential because it shapes how individuals perceive and interact with the world. It fosters a sense of personal responsibility and awareness, guiding smarter choices that consider long-term impacts on the planet and society. Cultivating this mindset encourages actions that contribute to a sustainable future, ensuring the well-being of both current and future generations.

ZHA Sustainability Mindset Values:

1. **Self-Awareness and Purposefulness**

    o   Understanding one's role in the interconnected web of life.

    o   Acting with a deep sense of purpose toward positive societal impact.

2. **Responsibility and Accountability**

    o   Taking ownership for personal, social, and environmental actions.

    o   Practicing ethical decision-making for long-term well-being.

3. **Respect for Nature and Diversity**

    o   Recognizing the intrinsic value of all forms of life.

o   Embracing cultural, ecological, and individual diversity as a strength.

4. **Continuous Learning and Adaptability**

   o   Staying open to change, growth, and evolving sustainable practices.

   o   Learning from failures and adapting quickly to challenges.

5. **Community-Centric Thinking**

   o   Prioritizing collective well-being over narrow self-interest.

   o   Building inclusive communities that support social and environmental justice.

6. **Innovation with Integrity**

   o   Solving problems creatively while respecting ethical boundaries.

   o   Ensuring innovations lead to genuine betterment, not harm.

7. **Minimalism and Mindful Consumption**

   o   Valuing simplicity and conscious use of resources.

   o   Reducing waste and promoting sustainable lifestyles.

8. **Empathy and Compassion**

   o   Deeply understanding and caring for the struggles of people and planet.

   o   Acting to alleviate suffering and promote dignity for all.

9. **Resilience and Courage**

   o   Facing adversity with strength and perseverance.

o   Challenging unsustainable norms with bold yet respectful actions.

10. **Long-Term Vision and Stewardship**

o   Thinking beyond the present moment to consider future generations.

o   Acting as stewards rather than exploiters of Earth's resources.

How to Apply Sustainability Values in Daily Life

Sustainability begins with small, everyday choices. Here are **practical ways** to adopt a sustainability mindset:

1. Reduce Waste and Use Resources Wisely

✓ Carry a **reusable water bottle and shopping bag** instead of plastic ones.
✓ Choose **digital books and notes** instead of printing paper unnecessarily.
✓ **Upcycle old clothes** instead of throwing them away.

2. Conserve Water and Energy

✓ **Turn off taps** while brushing your teeth to save water.
✓ **Switch off lights and fans** when leaving a room.
✓ **Use bicycles or walk** instead of taking cars for short distances.

3. Protect Nature and Biodiversity

✓ **Plant trees** and encourage green spaces in your school or neighborhood.
✓ **Avoid using chemical pesticides** that harm insects like bees and butterflies.
✓ **Do not litter**—keep your surroundings clean and inspire others to do the same.

4. Support Sustainable Brands and Local Businesses

✓ Buy products that are **environmentally friendly** and have **less plastic packaging**.
✓ Support **local farmers and organic food markets**.

5. Educate Yourself and Others

✓ Stay informed about **global sustainability issues** like climate change and pollution.
✓ Share **sustainability tips** on social media to spread awareness.

Our Ecosystem

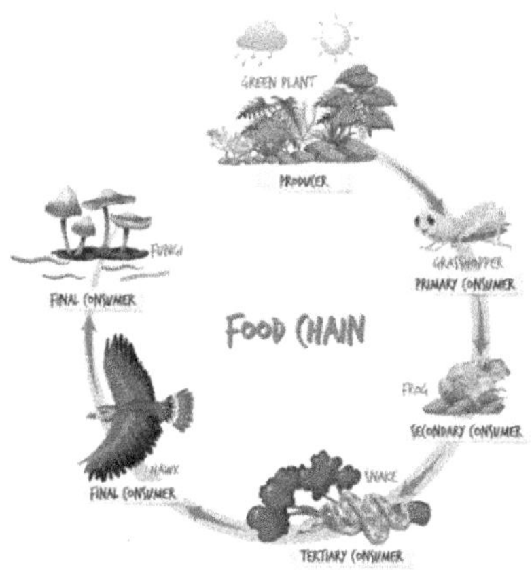

What is an Ecosystem?

An **ecosystem** is a community of living organisms (plants, animals, and microorganisms) interacting with their physical environment (air, water, soil, and climate). These interactions create a balanced system where each element plays a crucial role in maintaining ecological health.

Ecosystems can be **natural** (such as forests, rivers, and oceans) or **man-made** (such as urban parks and farmlands). Each ecosystem supports a unique variety of life forms adapted to its specific conditions.

Types of Ecosystems

1. **Forests**
   - Forests provide oxygen, store carbon, and support a diverse range of species.
   - Trees absorb CO_2, reducing climate change.
   - Example: The Amazon Rainforest, known as the "lungs of the Earth," produces about 20% of the world's oxygen.
2. **Oceans**
   - Cover over 70% of the Earth's surface and regulate global temperature.
   - Home to marine life such as fish, corals, and whales.
   - Play a key role in the water cycle and climate regulation.
3. **Rivers and Lakes**
   - Provide drinking water, irrigation, and habitats for aquatic organisms.
   - Carry nutrients that support biodiversity.
   - Example: The Ganges River in India supports millions of people and various wildlife.
4. **Urban Spaces**
   - Cities and towns where humans have altered the natural environment.
   - Urban ecosystems include parks, gardens, and green spaces that support birds, insects, and plant life.
   - Sustainable urban planning can help balance human needs with environmental conservation.

The Balance of Nature: Producers, Consumers, and Decomposers

Each ecosystem maintains a delicate **balance of nature**, where different organisms play specific roles.

1. Producers (Autotrophs)

- **Definition:** Organisms that make their own food using sunlight.
- **Examples:** Trees, grass, algae, and phytoplankton.
- **Role in the Ecosystem:** Convert sunlight into energy through photosynthesis, forming the base of the food chain.

2. Consumers (Heterotrophs)

- **Definition:** Organisms that cannot make their own food and must consume other organisms.

- **Types:**
    - **Herbivores** (Plant-eaters) – Cows, deer, caterpillars.
    - **Carnivores** (Meat-eaters) – Lions, eagles, sharks.
    - **Omnivores** (Both plant and meat-eaters) – Humans, bears, crows.
    - **Scavengers** (Eat dead animals) – Vultures, hyenas.

3. Decomposers (Recyclers)

- **Definition:** Organisms that break down dead matter and recycle nutrients into the soil.
- **Examples:** Fungi, bacteria, earthworms.
- **Role in the Ecosystem:** Help decompose organic material, enriching the soil for plants to grow.

Each group depends on the other, creating a **food web** that sustains life in the ecosystem.

How Human Activities Impact Ecosystems

Human actions can either **preserve** or **destroy** ecosystems. Some of the major threats to ecosystems include:

1. **Deforestation** – Cutting down forests for agriculture and urbanization destroys habitats and reduces oxygen production.

2. **Pollution** – Air, water, and soil pollution harm plants, animals, and human health.
3. **Overfishing** – Excessive fishing disrupts marine food chains, threatening ocean ecosystems.
4. **Climate Change** – Rising temperatures and extreme weather events disrupt natural habitats.
5. **Urbanization** – Expanding cities reduce green spaces, affecting biodiversity and water cycles.

Solution: Sustainable practices such as afforestation (planting trees), reducing waste, and protecting natural habitats can help restore ecosystem balance.

Waste Management – Reduce, Reuse, Recycle

What is Waste?

Waste is anything that is discarded, unwanted, or no longer useful. It comes from homes, schools, businesses, and industries. Proper waste management is essential to prevent pollution and conserve natural resources.

Types of Waste: Biodegradable & Non-Biodegradable

1. **Biodegradable Waste**
   - **Definition**: Waste that can break down naturally and decompose into the soil.
   - **Examples**: Food scraps, paper, leaves, vegetable peels, cotton, and wood.
   - **How it Decomposes**: Bacteria and fungi break it down, turning it into compost that nourishes the soil.

2. **Non-Biodegradable Waste**
   - **Definition**: Waste that does not decompose easily and remains in the environment for years.
   - **Examples**: Plastic bags, glass, metal, electronic waste, Styrofoam, and batteries.

  - **Impact**: If not properly managed, it can pollute land, water, and air.

The Journey of Waste: Where Does Our Garbage Go?

Ever wondered what happens after we throw our trash in the bin? Here's the journey of waste:

1. **Collection**
   - Garbage trucks collect waste from homes, schools, and offices.
2. **Sorting**
   - Waste is separated into **recyclables**, **compostable materials**, and **non-recyclables**.
3. **Processing**
   - Recyclable materials are sent to recycling plants.
   - Biodegradable waste is turned into compost or bio-gas.
   - Non-recyclable waste often goes to landfills or incineration centers.
4. **Final Disposal**
   - **Recyclables** are transformed into new products (e.g., paper, glass bottles).
   - **Compostable waste** enriches the soil.
   - **Non-recyclable waste** sits in landfills or is burned, sometimes releasing harmful gases.

Problem: Overfilled landfills pollute the environment. The solution? Practicing the **3Rs** to reduce waste.

The 3Rs: Reduce, Reuse, Recycle

1. Reduce (Use Less)

- Buy only what is needed to avoid waste.
- Choose products with minimal or biodegradable packaging.
- Use cloth bags instead of plastic bags.

2. Reuse (Use Again)

- Repurpose old clothes into bags or cleaning rags.
- Use glass jars to store food instead of buying new plastic containers.
- Donate old books, toys, and clothes instead of throwing them away.

3. Recycle (Make New from Old)

- Separate paper, plastic, metal, and glass for recycling.
- Buy recycled paper and eco-friendly products.
- Support brands that use sustainable packaging.

Daily Practices:

✓ Carry a reusable water bottle instead of buying plastic bottles.

✓ Use rechargeable batteries to reduce e-waste.

✓ Say NO to plastic straws and single-use plastics.

Plastic Pollution and Its Effects on Wildlife and Oceans

Plastic is **one of the biggest environmental threats** because it does not decompose easily. Instead, it breaks into microplastics that harm wildlife and humans.

How Plastic Affects the Environment:

- **Oceans**: Marine animals mistake plastic for food, leading to choking and starvation.

- **Birds**: Birds often get trapped in plastic waste, making it difficult for them to move or eat.
- **Soil & Water**: Plastic waste contaminates the environment, affecting plants, animals, and humans.

How to Reduce Plastic Waste?

- Use **cloth bags** instead of plastic.
- Carry a **steel or bamboo straw** instead of plastic straws.
- Avoid single-use plastics like forks, spoons, and plates.
- Participate in **clean-up drives** to remove plastic waste from local areas.

How Composting Helps Reduce Organic Waste

Composting is the process of turning food scraps and plant waste into **natural fertilizer**. It helps reduce landfill waste and improves soil quality.

Benefits of Composting:

✓ Reduces methane gas emissions from landfills.

✓ Enriches soil and helps plants grow better.

✓ Lowers the need for chemical fertilizers.

✓ Reduces the overall waste generated at home or school.

What Can You Compost?

✓ Fruit and vegetable peels

✓ Tea bags and coffee grounds

✓ Eggshells

✓ Dry leaves and grass clippings

✓ Paper towels and napkins

What NOT to Compost?

✓ Meat, fish, and dairy products (they attract pests)

✓ Plastic and metal

✓ Oily or greasy food

Home Activity: Make a DIY Compost Bin at Home or School

Objective: Learn how to compost and reduce organic waste.

Materials Needed:

✓ A large container or bucket (with small holes for airflow)

✓ Dry leaves or shredded paper

✓ Fruit and vegetable scraps

✓ Garden soil

✓ Water spray bottle

Steps to Create Your Compost Bin:

1. **Choose a Bin**: Take a bucket or container with a lid and drill small holes for airflow.
2. **Layering**: Start with a layer of dry leaves or shredded paper (carbon source).
3. **Add Food Waste**: Add fruit and vegetable peels, but avoid meat or dairy.
4. **Sprinkle Soil**: Helps in decomposing organic material.
5. **Moisten the Compost**: Use a spray bottle to keep it damp but not soggy.
6. **Turn the Compost**: Mix it every few days to allow airflow.

Results:

✓ In **2-3 months**, you will have **rich compost** to use in plants or gardens.

Biodiversity: Why Protecting Plants and Animals is Important

Biodiversity refers to the variety of life on Earth, including different species of plants, animals, and microorganisms.

Why is Biodiversity Important?

- **Ecosystem Stability:** A diverse range of species helps maintain ecological balance.
- **Food Security:** Many plants and animals provide food for humans.
- **Medicinal Resources:** Plants and microorganisms are used to develop medicines.
- **Climate Regulation:** Forests and oceans absorb CO_2, reducing global warming.

When species go **extinct**, ecosystems lose balance, affecting human survival. Protecting endangered species ensures a healthy planet for future generations.

Home Activity: Observe and Map a Mini-Ecosystem in Your School or Home Garden

Objective: To understand how different elements of an ecosystem interact.

Materials Needed: Notebook, pen, colored pencils, magnifying glass (optional).

Steps:

1. **Choose a Spot** – Pick a garden, park, or small natural space near your school or home.
2. **Identify Producers** – Look for plants, trees, or algae growing in the area.
3. **Spot Consumers** – Observe insects, birds, or small animals. What are they eating?

4. **Find Decomposers** – Look for earthworms, fungi, or rotting leaves.
5. **Sketch a Food Web** – Draw a simple diagram showing how different organisms interact.
6. **Record Observations** – Write down changes over time (e.g., new plants growing, animals visiting).

Discussion Questions:

- How does each organism contribute to the ecosystem?
- What human activities could affect this small ecosystem?
- How can we protect and enhance its biodiversity?

Water Management – Every Drop Counts

Understanding How Water Moves Around Us

The **water cycle** is nature's way of continuously recycling water. It ensures that water moves between the Earth's surface, atmosphere, and underground reserves.

Main Stages of the Water Cycle:

1. **Evaporation**
   - Heat from the sun turns water from oceans, lakes, and rivers into water vapor.

2. **Condensation**
   - As the water vapor rises, it cools and forms clouds.

3. **Precipitation**
   - When clouds become heavy with water, they release it as rain, snow, or hail.

4. **Collection (Runoff & Groundwater)**
   - Rainwater flows into rivers, lakes, and oceans. Some water seeps underground to become groundwater.

Why is the Water Cycle Important?

✓ It provides fresh water for drinking, agriculture, and industry.

✓ It maintains natural ecosystems.

✓ It helps regulate Earth's climate.

However, human activities like **deforestation, pollution, and excessive water use** can disrupt the water cycle, leading to water shortages and natural disasters.

The Importance of Clean Water for All Living Beings

Water is necessary for survival. Every organism, from tiny bacteria to humans, depends on water for various functions.

Why Clean Water is Important:

✓ **For Human Health:** Contaminated water spreads diseases like cholera and dysentery.

✓ **For Plants & Agriculture:** Crops need clean water to grow and produce food.

✓ **For Aquatic Life:** Fish and other marine species require unpolluted water to survive.

✓ **For Industries & Daily Life:** Water is used in manufacturing, cleaning, and electricity production.

Did You Know?

- **1 in 3 people** worldwide do not have access to safe drinking water.
- The **United Nations** recognizes clean water as a basic human right.

How Pollution Affects Water Bodies (Rivers, Lakes, Oceans)

Pollution is one of the biggest threats to water sources. Human activities contaminate water, making it unsafe for drinking, agriculture, and aquatic life

Main Causes of Water Pollution:

✓ **Industrial Waste** – Factories release toxic chemicals into rivers and lakes.

✓ **Sewage & Wastewater** – Improper disposal of human waste pollutes water bodies.

✓ **Agricultural Runoff** – Pesticides and fertilizers seep into water sources.

✓ **Plastic Pollution** – Plastic bottles and bags clog rivers and harm marine animals.

✓ **Oil Spills** – Accidents in the ocean release oil, destroying marine ecosystems.

Effects of Water Pollution:

✓ Causes deadly diseases and waterborne illnesses.

✓ Kills fish, turtles, and other aquatic life.

✓ Reduces the availability of fresh drinking water.

✓ Disrupts entire ecosystems.

✓ **Example:** The **Ganges River** in India is one of the most polluted rivers due to untreated sewage and industrial waste, yet millions depend on it for drinking and farming.

Saving Water at Home and School: Simple Habits That Make a Difference

How to Save Water at Home?

✓ **Turn off taps** while brushing your teeth or washing hands.

✓ **Take shorter showers** instead of long baths.

✓ **Use a bucket** instead of a running hose to wash cars or water plants.

✓ **Wash dishes in a filled sink** rather than under running water.

✓ **Fix leaks** – A dripping tap can waste **20 liters** of water per day!

How to Save Water at School?

✓ Educate students and teachers about water conservation.
✓ Install **water-efficient taps and toilets**.
✓ Plant **native trees** that require less water.
✓ Set up **rainwater harvesting** systems.

Fun Fact:

- A leaking tap that drips **once per second** can waste over **10,000 liters of water per year!**

Innovative Water Conservation Techniques

To tackle water scarcity, many innovative methods have been developed worldwide.

1. Rainwater Harvesting

- Collects rainwater from rooftops and stores it for later use.
- Used for watering plants, flushing toilets, and even drinking (after purification).

2. Drip Irrigation

- A method of watering plants by delivering water **directly to the roots**.
- Saves water compared to traditional flood irrigation.

3. Greywater Recycling

- Reuses water from sinks, showers, and washing machines for irrigation.
- Reduces fresh water consumption.

4. Desalination

- Removes salt from seawater to make it drinkable.
- Used in countries with limited freshwater resources (e.g., UAE, Israel).

Example:
The city of **Chennai, India**, has adopted rainwater harvesting in most homes to combat water shortages.

Home Activity: Design a "Save Water" Poster with Creative Solutions

Objective: Encourage students to think about water conservation creatively.

Steps to Create Your Poster:

1. **Title:** Choose a catchy phrase like **"Every Drop Counts"** or **"Save Water, Save Life"**.
2. **Illustrations:** Draw rivers, lakes, taps, and conservation methods (e.g., rainwater harvesting).
3. **Facts & Slogans:** Add interesting facts about water scarcity and pollution.
4. **Solutions:** Show simple ways to save water at home and school.
5. **Presentation:** Share your poster with classmates and teachers to spread awareness.

Bonus Challenge:
Make an **interactive poster** with moving parts or a **digital poster** using a computer!

Land and Soil Conservation – Caring for Our Earth

Soil is one of Earth's most valuable resources. It provides the foundation for plant growth, supports biodiversity, and helps regulate the climate. However, human activities like deforestation and unsustainable farming are leading to **soil erosion and land degradation**, making conservation efforts essential.

What is Soil, and Why is it Important?

Soil is the **top layer of the Earth's surface** where plants grow. It is made up of minerals, organic matter, air, and water, which provide nutrients and support for plants and animals.

Importance of Soil:

✓ **Supports Plant Growth** – Provides essential nutrients for crops, forests, and grasslands.
✓ **Stores Water & Filters Pollutants** – Helps purify water and prevent floods.
✓ **Home for Microorganisms & Insects** – Supports biodiversity and decomposes organic matter.
✓ **Regulates Climate** – Stores carbon, reducing greenhouse gases and controlling temperature.
✓ **Foundation for Human Settlements** – Used for agriculture, construction, and infrastructure.

 Fun Fact: It takes **500 years** to form just **2 cm** of topsoil, but poor practices can destroy it in a few years!

Causes of Soil Erosion and Land Degradation

Soil erosion occurs when the top layer of soil is **worn away** by wind, water, or human activities. When soil loses its nutrients and structure, it becomes degraded, making it difficult for plants to grow.

Main Causes of Soil Erosion:

1. Deforestation

- Cutting down trees exposes the soil, making it more vulnerable to wind and water erosion.

2. Overgrazing

- When too many animals feed on plants, they remove the protective vegetation cover, leading to soil loss.

3. Unsustainable Farming

- Excessive plowing and the use of chemical fertilizers degrade soil quality and kill beneficial microorganisms.

4. Construction & Urbanization

- Expanding cities replace fertile land with roads and buildings, reducing soil health.

5. Climate Change & Natural Disasters

- Heavy rainfall, floods, and droughts can accelerate erosion and soil degradation.

How Deforestation Affects Land and Climate

Deforestation is the large-scale clearing of forests for agriculture, logging, or urban expansion.

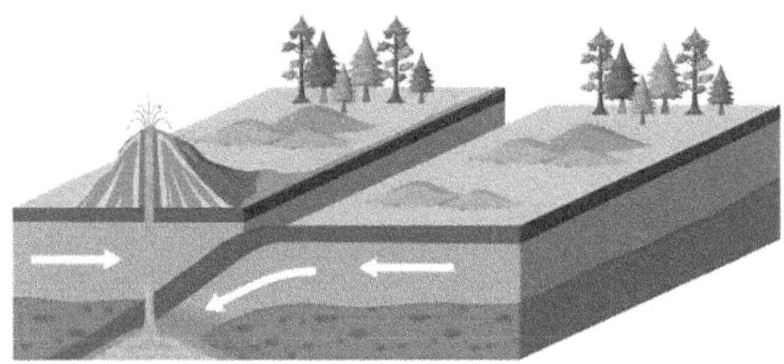

Effects on Land:

- **Loss of Topsoil** – Tree roots hold soil in place; when removed, soil erodes quickly.
- **Desertification** – Land becomes dry and barren, reducing its ability to support life.

Effects on Climate:

- **Increases Carbon Dioxide (CO_2) in the Atmosphere** – Trees absorb CO_2; without them, greenhouse gases increase, leading to global warming.
- **Disrupts Rainfall Patterns** – Forests regulate rainfall; cutting them down causes droughts or floods.
- **Reduces Oxygen Levels** – Fewer trees mean less oxygen production.

 Example: The Amazon Rainforest is called the "lungs of the Earth" because it produces **20% of the world's oxygen**. Deforestation there threatens global climate stability.

Sustainable Farming Practices

To protect soil and maintain its fertility, farmers use sustainable techniques that **preserve the land while growing food**.

1. Organic Farming

- Avoids chemical pesticides and fertilizers, using natural compost instead.
- Protects soil microbes that help plants grow.

2. Crop Rotation

- Growing different crops in the same field each season to prevent soil depletion.
- Helps maintain nutrient balance and reduces pests.

3. Agroforestry

- Planting trees alongside crops to provide shade, prevent soil erosion, and improve biodiversity.

4. Contour Plowing & Terracing

- Farming along the natural curves of hills to prevent water from washing soil away.
- Used in mountainous regions to conserve soil and water.

5. Cover Crops & Mulching

- Planting cover crops like clover or using dried leaves (mulch) to protect the soil from erosion.

Example: In India, organic farming in **Sikkim** has improved soil health and reduced pollution, making it a model for sustainable agriculture.

The Role of Trees and Plants in Protecting Soil

Trees and plants **act as natural protectors** of the soil, preventing erosion and improving fertility.

How Trees Help:

✓ **Roots Hold Soil Together** – Preventing it from being washed away by rain.
✓ **Increase Water Absorption** – Reducing surface runoff and conserving groundwater.
✓ **Provide Shade & Reduce Evaporation** – Keeping soil moist and fertile.
✓ **Drop Leaves That Turn Into Natural Fertilizer** – Improving soil nutrients.

 Example: In Africa's **Great Green Wall Project**, millions of trees are being planted to stop desertification in the Sahara region.

Home Activity: Plant a Tree and Track Its Growth Over Time

Objective:

Learn how trees improve soil, store carbon, and benefit the environment by planting and monitoring a sapling.

Materials Needed:

✓ A young plant or tree sapling
✓ A small shovel
✓ Watering can
✓ Notebook for observations

Steps:

1. **Choose a Location** – Find an area in your school, backyard, or community where the tree can grow.
2. **Plant the Tree** – Dig a hole, place the sapling inside, and cover the roots with soil.
3. **Water Regularly** – Keep the soil moist but not too wet.
4. **Observe and Record** – Measure its height and note changes in leaves or branches every week.
5. **Take a Photo Every Month** – Create a visual growth chart over time

Discussion Questions:

✓ How does the soil around your tree change over time?
✓ What animals or insects visit your tree?
✓ How does your tree help reduce air pollution and heat?

Bonus Challenge: Start a **"Green Club"** at school where students plant trees and track their environmental benefits!

Becoming a Young Sustainability Leader

Sustainability is not just about knowledge—it's about action! A **Young Sustainability Leader** is someone who applies sustainability principles & Values in daily life, inspires others, and leads initiatives to create a positive impact on the environment and society.

Leadership in sustainability is not limited to adults—many young people around the world have taken **bold steps** to protect nature, spread awareness, and drive meaningful change. You, too, can be part of this movement!

Key Message: "Every action, no matter how small, makes a difference."

Inspiring Stories of Young Sustainability Heroes Worldwide

Many young people have become **global changemakers** by taking sustainability into their own hands. Here are some inspiring examples:

1. Greta Thunberg (Sweden) – Climate Activist

- Started a **climate strike** at 15, inspiring millions to demand action from world leaders.
- Advocates for reducing carbon emissions to fight **global warming**.

2. Boyan Slat (Netherlands) – Ocean Cleanup Innovator

- At 18, he designed **The Ocean Cleanup**, a system to remove plastic waste from oceans.
- His project has removed **millions of tons** of plastic from the Pacific Ocean.

3. Autumn Peltier (Canada) – Water Protector

- Advocates for **clean water access** for Indigenous communities.
- Spoke at the **United Nations** about the importance of protecting water resources.

4. Vinisha Umashankar (India) – Solar-Powered Ironing Cart Innovator

- At 14, she invented a **solar-powered ironing cart** to replace charcoal-based ones.
- Won global recognition for her **eco-friendly invention**.

Key Lesson: Age doesn't matter—**passion and determination** can create real change!

Leading Projects in Your School and Community

You can be a **Young Sustainability Leader** by initiating or participating in **sustainability projects**. Here are some ideas:

1. Start a "Green Club via www.zspc.club " at School

- Organize **tree-planting drives** to make your campus greener.
- Set up a **recycling station** for paper, plastic, and e-waste.
- Educate students about **waste segregation and composting**.

2. Organize a Cleanup Drive

- Gather volunteers to clean up **parks, rivers, or beaches**.
- Educate people on **proper waste disposal**.

3. Reduce Plastic Use in Your School

- Request the school canteen to **avoid plastic straws and cups**.
- Encourage classmates to use **reusable lunch boxes and water bottles**.

4. Conduct Sustainability Workshops

- Teach students about the **importance of saving water and energy**.
- Invite local sustainability experts to speak.

5. Advocate for Sustainable Transportation

- Start a campaign promoting **cycling and walking** to school.
- Ask your school to provide **bicycle parking spaces**.

Key Lesson: Small actions, when done **together**, lead to **big results!**

How to Spread Awareness and Encourage Others

To make an impact, you need to **inspire and involve** others. Here's how:

1. Use Social Media for Good

✓ Share **eco-friendly tips** on Instagram, WhatsApp, or YouTube.
✓ Post pictures of **your sustainability projects** to motivate friends.
✓ Join **global sustainability challenges** like **#PlasticFreeJuly**.

2. Create Posters & Banners

✓ Design **"Save Water" or "Go Green"** posters for your school.
✓ Organize a **poster competition** to engage more students.

3. Organize an Event at School

✓ Hold a **"Zero-Waste Day"** where students use no plastic.
✓ Conduct a **sustainability quiz** to spread knowledge.

4. Lead by Example

✓ When others see **you** using a reusable bottle or planting trees, they'll follow!
✓ Speak about sustainability in **school assemblies or community meetings**.

 Key Lesson: Change starts with YOU! When you act, others will join.

Why Mindsets Matter for White Hat Certification?

A sustainability mindset is the foundation for creating a better future. It's about shifting from short-term convenience to long-term ecological balance, ensuring that our actions today don't compromise the well-being of future generations. This mindset is not just about knowing what's right—it's about doing what's right. It requires awareness, responsibility, and action. Let's explore the mindsets needed, how to build them, and the behaviors that align with sustainability principles.

Mindsets Required for Sustainability

1. Awareness and Being Conscious

- Mindset: Understand the interconnectedness of all life forms and ecosystems.

How to Build It:

- Educate Yourself: Learn about ecosystems, biodiversity, and the impact of human activities.
- Observe: Spend time in nature to appreciate its beauty and importance. Be mindful of the surroundings and be aware of what is in the present.
- Reflect: Regularly assess how your actions affect the environment.

Behavior:

- Reduce waste by recycling and composting.
- Conserve water and energy in daily life.
- Support conservation efforts and protect natural habitats.

2. Taking Responsibility

- Mindset: Take personal accountability for your environmental impact.

How to Build It:

- Track Your Impact: Use tools like carbon footprint calculators.
- Set Goals: Create personal sustainability goals (e.g., reduce plastic use, plant trees).
- Advocate: Encourage others to adopt sustainable practices.

Behavior:

- Avoid single-use plastics and opt for reusable alternatives.
- Participate in community cleanups and tree-planting drives.
- Educate others about the importance of sustainability.

3. Action-Oriented

- Mindset: Believe that small actions can lead to significant change.

How to Build It:

- Start Small: Begin with simple habits like turning off lights when not in use.
- Collaborate: Join or start sustainability initiatives in your community.
- Innovate: Find creative ways to reduce waste and conserve resources.

Behavior:

- Practice the 3Rs: Reduce, Reuse, Recycle.
- Support sustainable brands and local businesses.
- Advocate for policies that protect the environment.

How to Build These Mindsets

1. Education: Learn about sustainability principles and their real-world applications.

2. Practice: Start small—reduce waste, conserve water, and support sustainable practices.

3. Collaboration: Work with others to amplify your impact.

4. Reflection: Regularly assess your actions and their alignment with sustainability goals.

5. Advocacy: Share your knowledge and inspire others to adopt sustainable practices.

White Hat Certification Quiz & Final Reflection

To test your knowledge and commitment to sustainability, complete the **White Hat Certification Quiz**.

Quiz Topics:

1. What is a sustainability **mindset**?
2. How does **plastic pollution** affect oceans?
3. Name one **young sustainability leader** and their contribution.
4. List **three ways** to reduce waste at home.
5. What is the **importance of composting**?
6. How can **trees help prevent soil erosion**?
7. What is the **water cycle**, and why is it important?
8. Describe **one sustainability project** you would like to start in your school.

Reflection Questions:

- What is the most important thing you learned about sustainability?
- How will you apply sustainability principles in your daily life?
- What actions will you take to inspire others to be sustainable?

Final Challenge:

- Write a **"Sustainability Pledge"** and share it with your classmates.
- Set **personal sustainability goals** and track your progress.

Conclusion: Be the Change!

Being a Young Sustainability Leader means **taking responsibility for the planet**, inspiring others, and making a real impact. Whether it's **saving water, planting trees, reducing waste, or educating others**, every action counts.

"The Earth does not belong to us; we belong to the Earth. Let's protect it together!"

CHAPTER 2

Yellow HAT Certification (Basic - Level 1) - Principles of Sustainability Mindset, Energy, Recycling, Community Cleanups & Environmental Action

The Yellow HAT Certification under the ZHA Sustainability Mindset Practitioners Framework focuses on building fundamental awareness and practical skills in sustainability. This certification helps participants develop a proactive mindset toward environmental responsibility by integrating sustainability principles into daily life, education, and early professional development.

Overview: Yellow HAT Certification

Goal:

Key Learning Areas:

1. Understanding the Sustainability Mindset Principles – The shift from short-term convenience to long-term ecological balance.

2. Energy Efficiency & Renewable Resources – The basics of sustainable energy use and green technology.

3. Recycling & Waste Management – Reducing waste, upcycling, and developing circular economy habits.

4. Community Cleanups & Environmental Action – Taking personal responsibility and organizing community-driven initiatives.

Principles of Sustainability Mindset

Objective: Understand the core principles of sustainability mindset and apply them in personal, academic, and professional settings.

Key Concepts:
The psychology behind sustainable behavior – how habits shape from principles of sustainability mindset for a global environmental impact.

Goal:. This chapter emphasizes how simple changes in behavior can lead to massive global impact, fostering future leaders, entrepreneurs, and corporate sustainability champions.

1. Feeling Sufficient: Practicing Lean Thinking & Resource Sufficiency

✓ **Concept:** Learning to be content with what is necessary and avoiding overconsumption.
✓ **Application:** Encouraging minimalist living, lean business practices, and conscious consumerism.

Example:

- **Toyota's Lean Manufacturing System** – Toyota's **Kaizen (continuous improvement) and lean thinking** approach eliminates waste while maximizing efficiency.
- **Sweden's Lagom Philosophy** – The Swedish concept of **Lagom (just the right amount)** promotes balanced living and responsible consumption.

Practical Tip: Schools and workplaces can adopt **"Buy Only What You Need" campaigns** to promote **sufficiency over excess.**

2. Encouraging & Rewarding Sustainable Actions

Concept: Recognizing and celebrating contributions to sustainability while people are alive, ensuring that valuable individuals receive recognition at the right time.

Example:

- **The Goldman Environmental Prize** – A prestigious award given to grassroots environmental heroes **who take significant action** to protect nature.
- **ZSPC Club's "Sustainability Star of the Month"** – Students and professionals who actively participate in **green initiatives** are rewarded with **badges, certificates, or financial support** for further sustainability projects.

Practical Tip: Companies can implement a **"Green Employee of the Month"** program to encourage sustainable workplace practices.

3. Long-Term Thinking: Sustainable Decision-Making

Concept: Prioritizing **long-term benefits** over short-term profits, ensuring decisions positively impact the **environment, society, and economy.**

Example:

- **Norway's Sovereign Wealth Fund** – Norway invests its oil revenue into **renewable energy, education, and infrastructure**, ensuring wealth for future generations.
- **Patagonia's Business Model** – The outdoor apparel company **donates profits to environmental conservation** and designs **long-lasting** products to reduce waste.

Practical Tip: Introduce **"Future Impact Assessment" sessions** before making key financial or policy decisions in organizations.

4. Risk-Based Decision Making

Concept: Identifying and mitigating **environmental, social, and governance (ESG) risks** in sustainability strategies.

Example:

- **IKEA's Wood Sourcing Strategy** – IKEA only sources **FSC-certified wood**, reducing the risk of deforestation and ecosystem damage.
- **Google's Carbon Neutral Commitment** – Google **invests in renewable energy projects** to mitigate the environmental risks of energy consumption.

Practical Tip: Organizations can create a **Sustainability Risk Assessment Matrix** to evaluate projects before implementation.

5. Gender Equality: Promoting Diverse Perspectives & Equal Opportunities

Concept: Ensuring both men and women have **equal access** to sustainability leadership and opportunities.

Example:

- **UN's Sustainable Development Goal (SDG) 5 – Gender Equality** – The United Nations promotes **equal participation in sustainability initiatives**.
- **Tesla's Women in STEM Programs** – Encouraging **female engineers** to lead sustainable energy innovation.

Practical Tip: Companies can implement **gender-equal hiring policies and leadership training for women** in sustainability roles.

6. Sharing & Caring Collaboration for Sustainability

Concept: Fostering **collective action** to create **sustainable environmental and social solutions.**

Example:

- **The Ellen MacArthur Foundation's Circular Economy Model** – Encourages businesses to **collaborate in resource-sharing** to eliminate waste.

- **Community-Based Renewable Energy Projects in Germany** – Citizens co-own **solar and wind farms**, making clean energy a **shared responsibility**.

Practical Tip: Encourage **community-based sustainability projects** like **urban gardens, recycling hubs, and knowledge-sharing platforms.**

7. Environmental Stewardship: Responsibility for Nature

Concept: Protecting biodiversity, ecosystems, and natural resources.

Example:

- **India's Afforestation Drive** – Initiatives like **Cauvery Calling** encourage **tree planting** to restore forests.
- **Costa Rica's Carbon Neutrality** – The country has **protected rainforests** and relies on **99% renewable energy.**

 Practical Tip: Schools and businesses can implement **eco-challenges** like "Adopt-a-Tree" campaigns.

8. The Fail-Fast Approach in Vision Setting

Concept: Encouraging **innovation and rapid testing** to find the most effective sustainability solutions.

Example:

- **Tesla's Rapid Prototyping** – Tesla **quickly tests and adapts** new electric vehicle technologies, ensuring continuous improvement.
- **ZHA Foundation's Pilot Sustainability Programs** – Rolling out **small-scale sustainability initiatives** before large-scale implementation.

Practical Tip: Encourage **small-scale pilot sustainability projects** before full-scale implementation.

9. Community Engagement in Sustainability

Concept: Involving **local communities in decision-making** to ensure sustainability efforts align with their needs.

Example:

- **Coimbatore's Clean Water Initiative** – The local community and government worked together to **restore polluted water bodies**.
- **ZSPC's Organic Farmers League – Farmers and students collaborate** to promote sustainable farming.

Practical Tip: Organize **community-led sustainability events** such as clean-up drives, tree-planting days, or skill-sharing sessions.

10. Social Equality: Fair and Just Distribution of Resources

Concept: Ensuring sustainability efforts **do not exclude vulnerable communities**.

Example:

- **Bhutan's Gross National Happiness (GNH) Index** – Bhutan measures success by **people's well-being, not just economic growth**.
- **Fair Trade Certification for Farmers** – Ensures that **small farmers** receive **fair wages and sustainable working conditions**.

Practical Tip: Encourage businesses to **source materials from fair-trade certified suppliers**.

11. Continuous Learning & Improvement in Sustainability

Concept: Regularly **updating sustainability strategies** based on feedback, research, and technological advancements.

Example:

- **Harvard's Online Sustainability Courses** – Provides **continuous education on sustainability best practices.**
- **Google's Sustainable Data Centers** – Constantly **redesigns infrastructure** to minimize environmental impact.

Practical Tip: Implement **sustainability workshops and knowledge-sharing sessions** in workplaces.

12. Resource Conservation: Prioritizing Efficiency & Waste Reduction

Concept: Using resources **responsibly to minimize waste and environmental damage**.

Example:

- **Japan's Zero-Waste Town (Kamikatsu)** – A town where **residents sort waste into 45 categories** to maximize recycling.
- **The "Refill Revolution" in the UK** – Encourages citizens to **refill water bottles** instead of buying new plastic ones.

Practical Tip: Workplaces can implement a **"Bring Your Own Bottle & Mug"** policy to eliminate single-use plastics.

Conclusion: Building a Sustainable Future Through Values & Actions

By **adopting these principles**, individuals and organizations can drive **positive change at scale**. Whether through **education, policy, innovation, or**

grassroots action, these values create **a foundation for long-term sustainability.**

✓ The importance of individual and collective responsibility in sustainable life of all beings in this planet.
✓ How small changes create a large-scale impact (behavioral shift in consumer habits).

Activity:

- Sustainability Mindset Audit: Participants track their daily sustainable vs. unsustainable habits and suggest alternatives.

1. Energy Conservation & Renewable Energy

Objective: Introduce energy-efficient practices and explore renewable energy solutions to minimize carbon footprints.

Key Concepts:
✓ Understanding fossil fuels vs. renewables – why transition matters.
✓ How electricity consumption affects the environment and ways to reduce energy waste.
✓ Introduction to renewable energy sources: Solar, wind, hydro, and bio-energy.
✓ The impact of energy choices – How businesses and households can shift to sustainable energy practices.

Activity:

- Home Energy Audit: Identify power-intensive appliances, track energy use, and propose efficiency improvements.
- Green Innovation Challenge: Brainstorm creative renewable energy solutions for homes, schools, and communities.

2. Recycling & Waste Management

Objective: Build awareness of waste reduction, proper recycling methods, and the importance of the circular economy.

Key Concepts:
✓ Types of waste – Biodegradable vs. non-biodegradable materials.
✓ The waste hierarchy – Reduce, Reuse, Recycle, and Repurpose (4Rs).
✓ Plastic pollution and e-waste – How improper disposal harms ecosystems.
✓ Understanding the circular economy – How waste can be turned into valuable resources.

Activity:

- Community Recycling Project: Participants develop a household waste management plan and promote recycling practices.
- DIY Upcycling Workshop: Transform discarded items into reusable products (e.g., plastic bottle planters, paper recycling).

3. Community Cleanups & Environmental Action

Objective: Engage in hands-on sustainability initiatives to foster active participation in environmental conservation.

Key Concepts:
✓ The importance of community-driven environmental action – How grassroots movements create change.
✓ How pollution impacts communities – Case studies of waste mismanagement consequences.
✓ Planning and organizing cleanup events – Mobilizing groups for local impact.
✓ Long-term solutions – Encouraging businesses and schools to adopt sustainable waste management policies.

Activity:

- Neighborhood Cleanup Drive: Organize a local community cleanup (parks, beaches, school areas, etc.).

- Sustainability Pledge: Participants create a personal action plan to reduce waste and conserve energy over 6 months.

Energy, Energy Efficiency & Renewable Resources

The Basics of Energy, Sustainable Energy Use, and Green Technology

1. Understanding Energy: The Foundation of Sustainability

Energy is the driving force behind modern civilization. It powers homes, industries, and transportation. However, how we produce and consume energy significantly impacts our environment, economy, and social well-being.

Types of Energy:

✓ Primary Energy Sources – Natural resources like coal, oil, sunlight, and wind.

✓ Secondary Energy Sources – Electricity or hydrogen derived from primary sources.

✓ Renewable vs. Non-renewable Energy – The key difference lies in sustainability and replenishment over time.

Example: Fossil fuels (coal, oil, natural gas) take millions of years to form, whereas solar and wind energy are continuously available.

2. The Problem with Conventional (Non-Renewable) Energy Sources

Non-renewable energy sources—coal, oil, and natural gas—have powered economies for centuries, but they come with serious drawbacks:

✓ Carbon Emissions & Climate Change – Burning fossil fuels releases CO_2, contributing to global warming.

✓ Resource Depletion – Finite resources will eventually run out.

✓ Air & Water Pollution – Extracting and burning fossil fuels leads to toxic emissions, acid rain, and oil spills.

✓ Geopolitical Instability – Countries rich in oil/gas have political and economic power, leading to conflicts.

Example: The 1973 Oil Crisis highlighted global dependence on fossil fuels when oil prices skyrocketed due to supply restrictions.

3. Energy Efficiency: The First Step Toward Sustainability

Energy efficiency means getting the same output with less energy input. It is the most cost-effective and immediate way to reduce environmental impact.

Key Strategies for Energy Efficiency:
✓ Building Design: Energy-efficient homes and offices use proper insulation, LED lighting, and smart thermostats.
✓ Transportation: Electric vehicles (EVs), public transport, and cycling reduce fuel consumption.
✓ Industrial Processes: Smart manufacturing and automation minimize energy waste.
✓ Appliances & Devices: ENERGY STAR-rated appliances consume less electricity.

Example:

- Japan's "Cool Biz" Campaign encourages businesses to set AC at 28°C, saving electricity.
- The Empire State Building retrofit cut energy use by 38%, saving $4.4M annually.

4. Renewable Energy Sources: The Future of Clean Energy

Solar Energy: Power from the Sun

Solar power harnesses photovoltaic (PV) panels or solar thermal systems to generate electricity.

✓ Advantages: Infinite resource, low maintenance, and decreasing costs.
✓ Challenges: Weather-dependent, energy storage needed for nighttime use.

Example:

- India's Bhadla Solar Park is one of the world's largest solar farms (2.25 GW capacity).
- Tesla's Solar Roof Tiles seamlessly integrate into buildings for clean energy.

5. Wind Energy: Harnessing Nature's Power

Wind turbines convert kinetic energy from wind into electricity.

✓ **Advantages:** No emissions, scalable, cost-competitive.
✓ **Challenges:** Requires open land, wind inconsistency, bird migration impact.

Example:

- Denmark produces 50% of its electricity from wind power.
- Offshore wind farms like the UK's Hornsea Project maximize wind potential.

6. Hydropower: Energy from Water

Hydropower (dams, tidal, and wave energy) uses moving water to generate electricity.

✓ **Advantages:** Reliable, large-scale, supports energy storage.
✓ **Challenges:** Disrupts ecosystems, expensive to build.

Example:

- China's Three Gorges Dam is the largest hydroelectric plant, supplying 22500 MW.
- Iceland uses 100% renewable hydropower for electricity.

7. Biomass & Bioenergy: Power from Organic Matter

Burning organic material (wood, crops, waste) for energy.

✓ **Advantages:** Reuses waste, CO_2-neutral when managed properly.
✓ **Challenges:** Can lead to deforestation if not regulated.

Example:

- Sweden converts 99% of household waste into energy, reducing landfill waste.
- Biogas plants in India convert agricultural waste into clean cooking fuel.

8. Geothermal Energy: Earth's Inner Heat

Extracting heat from underground for electricity and heating.

✓ **Advantages:** Reliable, constant energy source.
✓ **Challenges:** Location-dependent, high initial costs.

Example:

- Iceland meets 90% of heating needs with geothermal energy.

9. Green Technology: Innovations for a Sustainable Future

✓ Smart Grids: Digital electricity networks that optimize supply and demand.
✓ Battery Storage: Tesla Powerwall & large-scale lithium-ion batteries store renewable energy.
✓ Hydrogen Fuel Cells: Clean alternative for transport & industrial energy

needs.

✓ Carbon Capture & Storage (CCS): Reducing CO_2 emissions from industries.

✓ Perovskite Solar Cells: New, cost-effective solar technology for wider adoption.

Example:

- Singapore's Floating Solar Farms reduce land usage for solar panels.
- AI-powered energy management systems optimize electricity use in cities.

10. Implementing Energy Sustainability in Daily Life

✓ Switch to Renewable Energy – Solar panels, green electricity providers.

✓ Use Energy-Efficient Appliances – LED lights, smart thermostats.

✓ Reduce Standby Power – Unplug devices when not in use.

✓ Optimize Transportation – Carpool, public transport, electric vehicles.

✓ Promote Sustainable Businesses – Support brands that use clean energy.

Example: Companies like Google & Apple run on 100% renewable energy.

Conclusion: The Road to a Clean Energy Future

Transitioning to sustainable energy requires collective effort from individuals, governments, and businesses. Investing in energy efficiency, renewable technologies, and green innovation ensures a future free from pollution, resource depletion, and climate risks.

Recycling – Reducing Waste, Upcycling, and Developing Circular Economy Habits

Introduction: Why Recycling is Important?

Recycling is a crucial part of sustainability, helping to reduce waste, conserve natural resources, and lower pollution levels. By transforming old materials into new products, recycling reduces the need for extracting raw materials, minimizes landfill waste, and cuts carbon emissions.

✓ Conserves Resources – Less demand for raw materials like trees, metals, and oil.
✓ Reduces Pollution – Less waste in oceans, landfills, and incinerators.
✓ Saves Energy – Recycling materials takes less energy than producing new ones.
✓ Encourages a Circular Economy – Keeps products and materials in use for as long as possible.

Example: Sweden has one of the highest recycling rates in the world, recycling 99% of its waste, with much of it turned into energy for homes.

1. Understanding Recycling: What Can Be Recycled?

Recyclable materials fall into different categories:

Paper & Cardboard

✓ Newspapers, magazines, office paper, books
✓ Cardboard boxes, paper bags

Example: Recycling one ton of paper saves 17 trees and reduces water pollution by 35%.

Plastic

✓ PET bottles, food containers, plastic bags (some types)
✓ Hard plastics like detergent bottles

Example: Adidas has produced over 50 million shoes from recycled ocean plastic, turning waste into fashion.

Metal

✓ Aluminum cans (soda, beer cans)
✓ Steel and copper wiring

Example: 75% of all aluminum ever produced is still in use today because of efficient recycling.

Glass

✓ Glass bottles and jars

Example: Recycling glass reduces energy consumption by 40% compared to making new glass.

Electronic Waste (E-Waste)

✓ Mobile phones, laptops, batteries
✓ Cables, electronic appliances

Example: Apple's Daisy robot dismantles 200 iPhones per hour to recover metals like gold and copper.

2. Reducing Waste – The First Step Towards Sustainability

✓ Buy only what you need – Avoid overconsumption.
✓ Choose products with minimal packaging – Reduce single-use plastics.
✓ Go digital – Use e-books, digital receipts, and online documents.
✓ Fix before replacing – Repair clothes, electronics, and furniture instead of discarding them.

Example: In France, a law requires companies to repair electronics for at least five years to reduce e-waste.

3. Upcycling – Giving Waste a New Life

Upcycling is creative reuse – transforming waste into higher-value products rather than discarding them.

✓ Old T-shirts → Reusable shopping bags
✓ Wine bottles → Decorative lamps

✓ Plastic bottles → Vertical gardens
✓ Old furniture → Modern home decor

Example: Nike's "Move to Zero" initiative turns old shoes into new sports gear.

4. Circular Economy – A Future Without Waste

A circular economy focuses on keeping materials in use instead of following the traditional "take-make-waste" model.

✓ Design for durability – Products should last longer.
✓ Encourage sharing models – Rental and second-hand markets.
✓ Turn waste into resources – Composting, biofuel, recycled fabrics.

Example: IKEA's Buy Back & Resell program allows customers to sell old furniture back to the company for resale or recycling.

5. How to Integrate Recycling into Daily Life

✓ Sort waste at home – Separate recyclables from trash.
✓ Use reusable items – Metal straws, cloth bags, glass jars.
✓ Join community recycling programs – Be part of clean-up drives.
✓ Support sustainable brands – Buy products made from recycled materials.
✓ Educate and spread awareness – Teach others about the benefits of recycling.

Example: The Ocean Cleanup Project removes plastic from the Great Pacific Garbage Patch, turning waste into recycled sunglasses for fundraising.

Conclusion: Recycling is Everyone's Responsibility

Recycling, upcycling, and embracing a circular economy can drastically reduce waste and protect the environment. Every small effort counts – the choices we make today will shape a more sustainable future for generations to come.

6. Community Cleanups & Environmental Action – Taking Personal Responsibility and Organizing Community-Driven Initiatives

Introduction: Why Community Cleanups Matter?

Community cleanups and environmental action are powerful ways to foster collective responsibility and encourage sustainable habits. These initiatives help restore public spaces, reduce pollution, and raise awareness about sustainability. Taking personal responsibility means recognizing the impact of our actions and actively contributing to a cleaner, greener future.

✓ Restores natural habitats – Protects wildlife and biodiversity.

✓ Reduces pollution – Prevents waste from harming ecosystems.

✓ Builds civic responsibility – Encourages teamwork and local engagement.

✓ Raises awareness – Educates people on waste management and environmental care.

✓ Promotes sustainable habits – Encourages long-term changes in behavior.

Example: The "Let's Do It! World Cleanup Day" movement mobilized over 180 countries and millions of volunteers to remove litter from cities, parks, and waterways.

1. Taking Personal Responsibility for a Cleaner Environment

Personal responsibility means adopting habits that contribute to a cleaner community and inspiring others to do the same.

✓ Proper Waste Disposal – Throwing trash in designated bins and separating recyclables.
✓ Saying No to Littering – Keeping public spaces clean.
✓ Reducing Plastic Usage – Choosing reusable bags, bottles, and containers.
✓ Eco-Friendly Transportation – Walking, cycling, or carpooling to reduce carbon footprints.
✓ Adopting Green Spaces – Maintaining gardens, planting trees, and supporting urban greening projects.

Example: In Japan, citizens carry their trash home when public bins are unavailable, keeping streets exceptionally clean.

2. Organizing Community Cleanups: A Step-by-Step Guide

A successful cleanup initiative requires planning, teamwork, and commitment.

Step 1: Identify the Cleanup Site

Find areas that need attention, such as:
✓ Beaches and riverbanks (plastic waste, fishing nets)
✓ Parks and playgrounds (litter, abandoned waste)
✓ Streets and markets (improperly discarded packaging)
✓ Forests and hiking trails (non-biodegradable waste)

Example: The "Clean Coasts" initiative in Ireland removed over 50,000 kg of marine litter from beaches with community support.

Step 2: Gather Volunteers and Resources

Engage local residents, schools, corporate employees, and environmental groups.

✓ Assign roles – Team leaders, logistics, waste collectors.
✓ Arrange supplies – Gloves, garbage bags, recycling bins, first-aid kits.
✓ Promote the event – Use social media, posters, and word-of-mouth.

Example: India's Swachh Bharat Mission mobilized millions of citizens to clean streets, turning it into a nationwide movement.

Step 3: Conduct the Cleanup Event

✓ Set safety guidelines – Use protective gear and avoid hazardous materials.
✓ Segregate waste – Separate recyclables from non-recyclables.
✓ Dispose of waste responsibly – Transport collected waste to appropriate facilities.
✓ Document and share impact – Take before-and-after photos, report results, and encourage future participation.

Example: Kenya banned plastic bags in 2017, leading to cleaner cities and inspiring community cleanups in Nairobi's rivers and slums.

3. Environmental Action Beyond Cleanups

Community action is not just about picking up trash—it involves long-term solutions for sustainable development.

Tree Planting & Reforestation

✓ Restores green cover and prevents soil erosion.
✓ Absorbs CO_2, reducing global warming.

Example: Ethiopia set a world record by planting 350 million trees in one day to combat deforestation.

Waste Management & Recycling Drives

✓ Encourages sorting waste into recyclables and non-recyclables.
✓ Educates communities on composting and circular economy models.

Example: The "Trash for Cash" program in the Philippines allows residents to exchange plastic waste for essential goods.

Water Conservation Campaigns

✓ Prevents water wastage and pollution.
✓ Promotes rainwater harvesting and responsible consumption.

 Example: Cape Town, South Africa, implemented strict water conservation measures to prevent a crisis during severe droughts.

Sustainable Transport Advocacy

✓ Promotes walking, cycling, and public transportation.
✓ Reduces air pollution and traffic congestion.

Example: In Bogotá, Colombia, Ciclovía Sundays close streets to cars, encouraging people to bike and walk instead.

Eco-Workshops & Awareness Campaigns

✓ Teaches sustainable habits like composting, upcycling, and minimalism.
✓ Encourages businesses to adopt green policies.

Example: Schools in Sweden have mandatory climate education, shaping environmentally responsible future generations.

4. The Power of Collaboration: Partnerships for Environmental Impact

Collaboration between citizens, businesses, and governments is key to long-term environmental success.

✓ Local Governments – Create policies and provide resources for sustainability projects.
✓ Schools & Colleges – Encourage students to participate in eco-friendly initiatives.
✓ Corporations – Invest in CSR projects related to waste management and green initiatives.
✓ Nonprofits & NGOs – Lead awareness campaigns and support grassroots action.

Example: The "Adopt-a-Highway" program in the USA allows businesses and volunteers to take responsibility for keeping highways clean.

5. How You Can Take Action Today?

✓ Join or start a local cleanup initiative.
✓ Reduce, reuse, and recycle in daily life.
✓ Educate friends and family on sustainable habits.
✓ Advocate for environmental policies in your community.
✓ Support businesses that follow sustainable practices.

Example: Greta Thunberg's climate activism started as a solo protest outside the Swedish Parliament and grew into a global movement for climate action.

How to Build These Mindsets

1. Education: Learn about sustainability principles and their real-world applications.

2. Practice: Start small—reduce waste, conserve energy, and support sustainable brands.

3. Collaboration: Work with others to amplify your impact.

4. Reflection: Regularly assess your actions and their alignment with sustainability goals.

5. Advocacy: Share your knowledge and inspire others to adopt sustainable practices.

Behaviors for Sustainability:

Energy Conservation

- Switch to renewables: Use solar panels or green energy providers.
- Optimize usage: Turn off lights and unplug devices when not in use.

- Promote efficiency: Use energy-efficient appliances and smart thermostats.

Recycling & Waste Management

- Sort waste: Separate recyclables from trash.
- Upcycle: Transform old items into new products.
- Support circular economy: Buy products made from recycled materials.

Community Cleanups

- Organize events: Plan cleanups for parks, beaches, or streets.
- Educate: Teach others about proper waste disposal.
- Advocate: Push for policies that reduce waste and pollution.

Environmental Action

- Plant trees: Restore green cover and combat climate change.
- Conserve water: Fix leaks and use water-efficient appliances.
- Reduce plastic: Avoid single-use plastics and support bans.

Conclusion: Small Actions Lead to Big Change

A clean and healthy environment begins with individual responsibility and collective action. Whether it's organizing a beach cleanup, planting trees, or advocating for better waste management, every effort contributes to a more sustainable world.

Chapter 3:

Blue HAT Certification (Basic - Level 1) (Basic - Level 1) - ZHA Sustainability Mindset Practitioner's Framework, Sustainable Transportation, Water Conservation, Social Equity

ZHA Sustainability Mindset Practitioner's Framework

Goal of the Blue HAT Certification

The Blue HAT Certification is designed to instill foundational knowledge and practical skills in sustainability, focusing on three key areas:
1. ZHA Sustainability Mindset Practitioner's Framework
2. Sustainable Transportation – Reducing carbon footprints and promoting eco-friendly mobility solutions.
3. Water Conservation – Encouraging responsible water use and preservation of global water resources.
4. Social Equity – Ensuring fairness, inclusion, and equal opportunities in sustainability initiatives.

This certification equips individuals with the mindset to become responsible global citizens, leaders, and change-makers, enabling them to apply sustainability principles in their daily lives, workplaces, and communities.

ZHA Sustainability Mindset Practitioner's Framework

The ZHA Framework for sustainability mindset development is based on four key pillars that derives the focus areas of the Twelve ZHA Sustainability Mindset Maturity Certifications of Four ZHA Sustainability Mindset Maturity Levels:

✓ People – Fostering inclusivity, equity, and well-being for all.
✓ Prosperity – Ensuring economic growth aligns with social and environmental responsibility.

✓ Partnership – Promoting collaboration between individuals, organizations, and communities for a shared sustainable future.
✓ Planet – Protecting and restoring the environment to maintain balance in ecosystems.

This framework ensures that sustainability is approached holistically, integrating these four essential elements into all decision-making processes.

Sustainable Transportation – Moving Towards a Greener Future

Why Sustainable Transportation Matters?

Transportation is a major contributor to carbon emissions and climate change. Sustainable mobility focuses on reducing reliance on fossil fuels and adopting greener, more efficient alternatives.

✓ Reduces Air Pollution (Planet) – Lowers greenhouse gas emissions.
✓ Saves Energy & Resources (Prosperity) – Decreases dependence on non-renewable fuels.
✓ Promotes Healthier Lifestyles (People) – Encourages walking, cycling, and public transport.
✓ Decreases Traffic Congestion (Partnership) – Improves urban mobility through collective efforts.

Examples of Sustainable Transportation Solutions

- Public Transport – Metro, buses, and shared mobility services.
- Electric Vehicles (EVs) – Reducing carbon footprints through cleaner fuel alternatives.
- Cycling & Walking – Promoting bike lanes and pedestrian-friendly infrastructure.
- Carpooling & Ride-Sharing – Reducing the number of individual vehicles on roads.
- Green Logistics – Using eco-friendly delivery methods and sustainable supply chains.

Example: The Netherlands has more bicycles than people, reducing emissions and improving public health.

Example: Norway aims to have 100% electric cars by 2025, leading global EV adoption.

Example: India's Delhi Metro is one of the world's first metro systems to be powered by solar energy.

Water Conservation – Protecting Our Most Precious Resource

Why Water Conservation is Critical?

Water is a finite resource, yet it is being depleted at an alarming rate due to pollution, overuse, and climate change. Sustainable water management ensures availability for future generations.

✓ Prevents Water Scarcity (People) – Ensures clean drinking water access for all.
✓ Supports Agriculture & Food Security (Prosperity) – Conserves irrigation water for farming.
✓ Reduces Energy Consumption (Partnership) – Saves energy used for water extraction and purification.
✓ Protects Aquatic Ecosystems (Planet) – Maintains biodiversity in lakes, rivers, and oceans.

Water Conservation Strategies

- Rainwater Harvesting – Capturing and storing rainwater for later use.
- Greywater Recycling – Reusing water from sinks, showers, and washing machines.

- Efficient Irrigation – Using drip irrigation to reduce water wastage in agriculture.
- Fixing Leaks – Reducing water loss from pipes and fixtures.
- Sustainable Water Policies – Encouraging laws to prevent over-extraction of water resources.

Example: In Singapore, the NEWater project recycles wastewater into drinking water, ensuring long-term water security.

Example: In Rajasthan, India, traditional stepwells are being revived to recharge groundwater.

Example: In California, strict water-saving regulations have reduced per capita water consumption by 25%.

Social Equity – Ensuring Fairness and Inclusion in Sustainability

Why Social Equity is Essential?

Sustainability is not just about the environment—it is about creating fair opportunities for all. Social equity ensures that economic, environmental, and social benefits are distributed fairly across all communities, regardless of gender, income, or background.

✔ Reduces Poverty & Inequality (People) – Ensures access to education, healthcare, and sustainable livelihoods.
✔ Empowers Marginalized Communities (Prosperity) – Provides resources and opportunities for underprivileged groups.
✔ Encourages Inclusive Decision-Making (Partnership) – Involves all voices in sustainability discussions.
✔ Promotes Gender Equality (Planet) – Supports women and minority representation in sustainability initiatives.

Examples of Social Equity in Sustainability

- Fair Wages & Labor Rights – Ensuring workers in green industries receive fair compensation.
- Inclusive Urban Planning – Designing sustainable cities with accessible public spaces.

- Equal Access to Clean Energy & Water – Providing affordable solar and water solutions to rural areas.
- Education & Skill Development – Training underserved communities in sustainability professions.
- Diversity & Inclusion in Leadership – Encouraging equal representation in corporate sustainability roles.

Example: Rwanda has the highest percentage of women in parliament (over 60%), ensuring inclusive policy making.

Example: India's Self-Employed Women's Association (SEWA) empowers women through sustainable livelihoods.

Example: Companies like Patagonia and Ben & Jerry's incorporate ethical labor practices and social impact initiatives into their business models.

Examples of Mindsets Required for this Certification of Sustainability are,

1. Holistic Thinking Mindset (ZHA Framework)

- Mindset: Understand that sustainability is interconnected—people, prosperity, partnership, and planet are all linked.

- **How to Build It:**

  - Learn the Framework: Study the ZHA Sustainability Mindset Practitioner's Framework and its four pillars.

  - Think Systemically: Consider how your actions impact all four pillars.

  - Reflect: Regularly assess how your decisions align with holistic sustainability.

- **Behaviour:**

  - Advocate for policies that balance economic growth with environmental protection.

○ Support initiatives that promote social equity and
environmental health.

2. Eco-Friendly Mobility Mindset (Sustainable Transportation)

- Mindset: Prioritize low-carbon, efficient, and inclusive transportation
solutions.

- **How to Build It:**

  ○ Educate Yourself: Learn about the environmental impact of
  transportation.

  ○ Adopt Green Habits: Start using public transport, cycling, or
  carpooling.

  ○ Advocate: Push for better infrastructure for sustainable
  mobility.

- **Behavior:**

  ○ Use electric vehicles or public transport.

  ○ Support policies that promote bike lanes and pedestrian-
  friendly cities.

3. Water Stewardship Mindset (Water Conservation)

- Mindset: Treat water as a precious, finite resource that must be
conserved.

- **How to Build It:**

  ○ Understand Water Scarcity: Learn about global water
  challenges.

  ○ Practice Conservation: Fix leaks, use water-efficient
  appliances, and reduce waste.

  ○ Innovate: Explore rainwater harvesting and greywater
  recycling.

- **Behavior:**

  - Install water-saving devices at home.

  - Participate in community water conservation projects.

4. Equity and Inclusion Mindset (Social Equity)

- Mindset: Ensure that sustainability benefits everyone, especially marginalized communities.

- **How to Build It:**

  - Educate Yourself: Learn about social equity issues and their connection to sustainability.

  - Advocate for Fairness: Support policies that promote equal access to resources.

  - Empower Others: Mentor or support underrepresented groups in sustainability initiatives.

- **Behavior:**

  - Support fair-trade and ethical brands.

  - Volunteer for programs that provide clean water or energy to underserved communities.

How to Build These Mindsets

1. Education: Learn about sustainability principles and their real-world applications.

2. Practice: Start small—use public transport, conserve water, and support fair practices.

3. Collaboration: Work with others to amplify your impact.

4. Reflection: Regularly assess your actions and their alignment with sustainability goals.

5. Advocacy: Share your knowledge and inspire others to adopt sustainable practices.

Behaviors for Sustainability

Sustainable Transportation

- Switch to green mobility: Use electric vehicles, public transport, or bicycles.

- Reduce car dependency: Carpool or use ride-sharing services.

- Advocate for change: Push for better public transport and cycling infrastructure.

Water Conservation

- Fix leaks: Repair dripping taps and pipes to save water.

- Use efficient appliances: Install low-flow showerheads and dual-flush toilets.

- Harvest rainwater: Collect and store rainwater for non-potable uses.

- Educate others: Teach your community about water-saving techniques.

Social Equity

- Support fair wages: Buy from brands that ensure fair labor practices.

- Promote inclusion: Advocate for policies that ensure equal access to resources.

- Empower communities: Support education and skill development programs for marginalized groups.

Blue HAT Certification: The Path Forward

What Participants Will Learn?

✓ How to adopt sustainable transportation practices and advocate for green mobility.

✓ Methods to conserve water and implement responsible water use in daily life.

✓ The importance of social equity in sustainability and ways to promote fairness and inclusion.

✓ Real-world case studies and success stories of sustainable innovations.

✓ Practical ways to implement the ZHA Sustainability Mindset Practitioner's Framework based on People, Prosperity, Partnership, and Planet.

Who Should Take This Certification?

✓ Students and young professionals interested in sustainability.

✓ Corporate employees looking to integrate green practices in their workplaces.

✓ Community leaders and activists promoting social and environmental justice.

✓ Entrepreneurs and policymakers working on sustainable solutions.

Impact of the Certification

✓ Creates responsible sustainability practitioners.

✓ Empowers individuals to take meaningful environmental and social action.

✓ Builds a network of leaders committed to long-term sustainability goals.

✓ Encourages global collaboration for sustainable development.

Conclusion: Be the Change with the Blue HAT Certification

By achieving the Blue HAT Certification, individuals not only gain knowledge but become leaders in sustainability. Sustainable transportation, water conservation, and social equity are critical components in shaping a just and environmentally responsible world.

CHAPTER 4

Green HAT Certification (Basic - Level 1) -United Nation - SDG Alignment with Sustainability Mindset Framework, Wildlife Conservation, Preserving Aquatic Life, Restoration of Habitats

U.N SDG Alignment with the ZHA Sustainability Mindset Framework

Goal of the Green HAT Certification

The **Green HAT Certification** is designed to **instill environmental stewardship** by focusing on four key areas:

1. United Nations' SDG Alignment with Sustainability Mindset Framework -Being aware of the global sustainability goals being met through the pathway practices of Sustainability Mindset Framework

2. Wildlife Conservation – Protecting endangered species and preserving biodiversity

3. Preserving Aquatic Life – Ensuring the health of marine and freshwater ecosystems.

4. Restoration of Habitats – Rehabilitating degraded environments to sustain biodiversity.

This certification aligns with the **United Nations Sustainable Development Goals (SDGs)** and the **ZHA Sustainability Mindset Practitioner's Framework**, equipping individuals with the mindset and skills to **contribute to a healthier planet** through action and advocacy.

U.N SDG Alignment with ZHA Sustainability Mindset Framework

The **Green HAT Certification** integrates **U.N Sustainable Development Goals (SDGs)** with the **ZHA Sustainability Mindset Practitioner's Framework** by emphasizing:

The **United Nations Sustainable Development Goals (SDGs)** are a universal blueprint for achieving a better and more sustainable future for all. These **17 goals** address global challenges such as poverty, inequality, climate change, environmental degradation, and justice.

The **ZHA Sustainability Mindset Framework (SMF)** is built on four core pillars: **People, Prosperity, Partnership, and Planet**. These pillars align with the **SDGs** by fostering a mindset that integrates **sustainability into daily life, decision-making, and leadership**.

Developing a **Sustainability Mindset** means **not only understanding global challenges** but also **adopting practices that contribute to achieving these goals** in a way that is measurable and impactful at personal, community, corporate, and global levels.

How the ZHA Sustainability Mindset Framework Aligns with SDGs?

1. People (Social Responsibility & Well-being) → SDGs 1, 2, 3, 4, 5, 10

- **Goal 1: No Poverty** – Encouraging sustainable economic models to reduce poverty.
- **Goal 2: Zero Hunger** – Promoting sustainable agriculture and food security.
- **Goal 3: Good Health and Well-being** – Encouraging clean environments, mental well-being, and healthcare access.
- **Goal 4: Quality Education** – Integrating sustainability education into learning institutions.

- **Goal 5: Gender Equality** – Encouraging diverse and inclusive leadership and workplaces.
- **Goal 10: Reduced Inequalities** – Ensuring fair distribution of resources and opportunities.

Example: Implementing **community-driven education programs** that teach sustainable agriculture to rural farmers, aligning with **SDG 2 (Zero Hunger)** while promoting **SDG 4 (Quality Education)**.

2. Prosperity (Economic Growth & Innovation) → SDGs 7, 8, 9, 11, 12

- **Goal 7: Affordable and Clean Energy** – Transitioning to renewable energy sources and increasing energy efficiency.
- **Goal 8: Decent Work and Economic Growth** – Encouraging sustainable businesses and green jobs.
- **Goal 9: Industry, Innovation, and Infrastructure** – Promoting sustainable industrialization and resilient infrastructure.
- **Goal 11: Sustainable Cities and Communities** – Developing green infrastructure and efficient urban planning.
- **Goal 12: Responsible Consumption and Production** – Encouraging circular economy practices.

Example: Encouraging companies to integrate **energy-efficient technologies** and **adopt circular economy models** (e.g., **recycling industrial waste** into new materials) contributes to **SDG 12 (Responsible Consumption & Production)** and **SDG 9 (Industry, Innovation & Infrastructure)**.

3. Partnership (Collaboration & Collective Action) → SDGs 16, 17

- **Goal 16: Peace, Justice, and Strong Institutions** – Promoting ethical leadership and transparency.
- **Goal 17: Partnerships for the Goals** – Strengthening cooperation between governments, corporations, NGOs, and individuals.

Example: Public-private partnerships that encourage sustainability-driven projects (e.g., government incentives for corporations adopting **net-zero carbon policies**) align with **SDG 17 (Partnerships for the Goals)**.

4. Planet (Environmental Stewardship) → SDGs 6, 13, 14, 15

- **Goal 6: Clean Water and Sanitation** – Ensuring responsible water management and conservation.
- **Goal 13: Climate Action** – Reducing carbon footprints and mitigating climate risks.
- **Goal 14: Life Below Water** – Protecting oceans and marine ecosystems.
- **Goal 15: Life on Land** – Restoring forests, protecting biodiversity, and conserving ecosystems.

Example: Implementing **tree-planting initiatives** and **water conservation programs** in communities contributes to **SDG 15 (Life on Land)** and **SDG 6 (Clean Water and Sanitation)**.

The Pathway Practices of Sustainability Mindset Framework in Achieving SDGs

To bridge **awareness and action**, the **Sustainability Mindset Framework** includes **pathway practices**—practical, real-world applications that ensure individuals and organizations can actively contribute to **achieving the SDGs** through sustainable thinking and behavior.

✓ **Key Practices for Aligning with SDGs**

1. Sustainable Decision-Making – Encouraging individuals to think long-term, considering environmental and social impact before making economic or lifestyle decisions.

Example: Companies adopting **risk-based decision-making** for sustainable investments instead of short-term profit-driven choices.

2. Resource Sufficiency Mindset – Understanding that excessive consumption depletes natural resources.
Example: Promoting **minimalist lifestyles** to reduce waste and energy usage.

3. Circular Economy Approach – Reducing waste by reusing, recycling, and upcycling materials.
Example: Fashion brands adopting **zero-waste production** to reduce textile waste in landfills.

4. Community Engagement & Empowerment – Encouraging grassroots movements for sustainability action.
Example: Local communities organizing **waste management and cleanup drives** to support **SDG 11 (Sustainable Cities & Communities)**.

5. Collaboration Across Sectors – Strengthening **corporate-social partnerships** to scale sustainability solutions.
Example: Tech companies investing in **renewable energy projects** to reduce carbon footprints.

✓ **Conclusion: Why This Matters?**

By aligning with the **United Nations' SDGs**, the **ZHA Sustainability Mindset Framework** transforms sustainability from a **concept into daily practice**. It ensures that individuals, communities, and businesses:

✓ **Adopt a sustainable mindset** by integrating SDG-focused behaviors into everyday life.
✓ **Foster innovation and resilience** by applying sustainability practices in industries, education, and governance.
✓ **Drive long-term impact** by shaping future leaders who think beyond economic gain and prioritize **People, Prosperity, Partnership, and Planet**.

Wildlife Conservation – Protecting Biodiversity

Why Wildlife Conservation Matters?

Wildlife plays a crucial role in **maintaining ecological balance**. However, habitat destruction, poaching, and climate change threaten biodiversity, leading to species extinction. Conservation efforts ensure that animals, birds, and plants continue to thrive for future generations.

✓ **Protects Endangered Species** (Planet) – Prevents extinction and ensures biodiversity.
✓ **Preserves Ecosystem Functions** (Prosperity) – Wildlife supports natural processes like pollination, seed dispersal, and pest control.
✓ **Sustains Livelihoods** (People) – Eco-tourism and conservation create jobs and economic opportunities.
✓ **Encourages Ethical & Legal Protections** (Partnership) – Strengthens global laws against wildlife trafficking.

✓ **Protects Endangered Species (Planet) – Prevents Extinction and Ensures Biodiversity**

Why Protecting Endangered Species is Crucial?

Biodiversity is the foundation of a healthy planet. Each species plays a critical role in **maintaining ecological balance**, from pollinating plants to controlling pests and maintaining the food chain. However, **human activities**—such as deforestation, poaching, climate change, and pollution—have accelerated the extinction of many species.

Protecting endangered species is essential because:
✓ It **preserves biodiversity**, ensuring that ecosystems remain resilient.

✓ It **maintains ecological balance**, preventing disruptions in the food chain.
✓ It **sustains human livelihoods**, especially for communities dependent on nature for food, medicine, and economic activities like tourism.
✓ It **helps combat climate change**, as species like forests and marine life contribute to carbon absorption and oxygen production.

Causes of Species Endangerment

1. Habitat Destruction – Deforestation, urban expansion, and agriculture lead to habitat loss.
2. Illegal Wildlife Trade – Poaching and trafficking of animals for fur, ivory, and exotic pet trade.
3. Climate Change – Rising temperatures, changing weather patterns, and melting ice caps threaten species like polar bears and corals.
4. Pollution – Water and air pollution poison habitats, affecting species survival.
5. Invasive Species – Non-native species introduced to an environment can outcompete native species.

✓ Strategies for Protecting Endangered Species

1. Establishing Wildlife Sanctuaries and National Parks

Protected areas provide a **safe haven for endangered species** by restricting hunting, deforestation, and habitat destruction.

Example: The **Sundarbans National Park** in India protects the endangered **Royal Bengal Tiger**, ensuring their population does not decline further.

Example: The **Yellowstone National Park** in the USA helped recover **Gray Wolves**, which were reintroduced after being hunted to near extinction.

2. Anti-Poaching and Wildlife Protection Laws

Governments enforce laws to **combat poaching and illegal wildlife trade**. Strengthening penalties for poachers and traffickers helps deter illegal activities.

Example: The **Convention on International Trade in Endangered Species (CITES)** regulates and bans the trade of endangered animals and their body parts, such as ivory from elephants and rhino horns.

Example: China banned the **commercial trade of pangolins**, the most trafficked mammal in the world, to help prevent their extinction.

3. Captive Breeding and Reintroduction Programs

Scientists and conservationists breed endangered animals in captivity and **release them into their natural habitats** to increase their numbers.

Example: The **Giant Panda** population recovered due to China's **captive breeding programs**, leading to the species being reclassified from "Endangered" to "Vulnerable."

Example: The **California Condor**, once nearly extinct with only 27 individuals left in 1987, was bred in captivity and successfully reintroduced to the wild.

4. Community Involvement and Education

Educating local communities and involving them in **wildlife conservation programs** ensures sustainable protection efforts. Eco-tourism also provides financial incentives to protect wildlife.

Example: The **Maasai community in Kenya and Tanzania** plays a role in protecting lions through the **Lion Guardians Program**, turning former lion hunters into conservationists.

Example: In India, the **Snow Leopard Conservation Program** engages local communities in protecting the endangered **Snow Leopard** while promoting eco-tourism.

5. Climate Action to Preserve Habitats

Addressing climate change is essential to **protect species threatened by rising temperatures**. Restoring forests, reducing carbon emissions, and preserving wetlands help sustain natural habitats.

Example: The **Great Green Wall** in Africa is restoring forests and preventing desert expansion, helping save species like the African Elephant.

Example: The **Coral Reef Restoration Program** in Australia is helping to protect the **Great Barrier Reef**, a crucial marine habitat for thousands of species.

Conclusion: Why It Matters

Protecting endangered species is not just about saving individual animals—it's about preserving **entire ecosystems** that sustain life on Earth. By **creating safe habitats, enforcing strict laws, restoring natural environments, and involving local communities**, we can **prevent extinctions and maintain biodiversity for future generations**.

Preserving Aquatic Life – Saving Oceans, Rivers, and Lakes

Why Preserving Aquatic Life is Crucial?

Oceans and freshwater bodies provide food, oxygen, and climate regulation, but they are endangered due to pollution, overfishing, and habitat destruction. Protecting aquatic life ensures that **marine and freshwater ecosystems** remain viable for future generations.

✓ **Maintains Biodiversity** (Planet) – Prevents marine species from becoming extinct.
✓ **Ensures Sustainable Fishing** (Prosperity) – Regulates fishing practices to prevent depletion of marine resources.
✓ **Reduces Pollution & Plastic Waste** (People) – Prevents toxins from entering the food chain.
✓ **Encourages Global Cooperation** (Partnership) – International agreements to prevent overfishing and ocean degradation.

Strategies for Preserving Aquatic Life

- **Reducing Plastic Pollution** – Banning single-use plastics and promoting recycling.
- **Marine Protected Areas (MPAs)** – Designating regions where fishing and industrial activities are restricted.
- **Sustainable Fishing Practices** – Implementing quotas and bans on overfishing.
- **Coral Reef Restoration** – Protecting coral reefs from climate change and ocean acidification.

- **Water Pollution Control** – Reducing industrial waste discharge into water bodies.

 Example: The **Great Barrier Reef Protection Program** in Australia has helped preserve coral reefs by limiting human activity and controlling pollution.

Example: Norway and Iceland practice **sustainable fisheries management**, ensuring fish populations are not overexploited.

Example: The **Ocean Cleanup Project** has removed over **5,000 tons of plastic** from the Pacific Garbage Patch, reducing ocean pollution.

✔ **Key Benefits of Preserving Aquatic Life**

1. Biodiversity Conservation – Protecting Marine & Freshwater Species

Why It Matters:

- Oceans and freshwater bodies are home to **over 80% of the planet's life forms**.
- Coral reefs alone support **25% of marine species**, making them one of the most diverse ecosystems on Earth.
- Protecting aquatic life prevents species extinction and maintains genetic diversity, which is crucial for ecosystem resilience.

Example:

- **Marine Protected Areas (MPAs)**, such as the Great Barrier Reef, help endangered species like **sea turtles, dolphins, and sharks** recover by restricting human activities like overfishing and pollution.
- **River restoration projects**, like cleaning up the Ganges River in India, help protect freshwater species like the endangered **Ganges river dolphin**.

2. Ensuring Clean Water for Human & Ecosystem Health

Why It Matters:

- Healthy aquatic ecosystems **naturally filter pollutants** and provide clean water for drinking, agriculture, and industry.
- Polluted rivers and lakes lead to waterborne diseases, impacting human health.

Example:

- **Wetlands** act as natural filters by trapping pollutants, improving water quality before it reaches rivers and lakes.
- **Mangrove forests** in coastal areas filter out harmful substances before they reach the ocean, protecting marine life from toxic waste.

3. Climate Regulation – Oceans as Carbon Sinks

Why It Matters:

- Oceans **absorb 30% of the world's CO_2 emissions**, helping to mitigate climate change.
- Marine ecosystems, such as **seagrass meadows and mangroves**, store **up to 10 times more carbon per hectare** than terrestrial forests.

Example:

- Protecting **seagrass beds** in places like Florida and the Mediterranean reduces CO_2 in the atmosphere, slowing global warming.
- Restoring **coral reefs** enhances carbon sequestration and protects coastlines from extreme weather events like hurricanes.

4. Sustainable Fisheries & Food Security

Why It Matters:

- **3 billion people** rely on seafood as their primary protein source.
- Overfishing and habitat destruction threaten global food security and local economies.

Example:

- Sustainable fishing practices, like using **eco-friendly fishing nets and marine sanctuaries**, prevent overfishing and allow fish populations to replenish.
- Community-led conservation projects, like **Indonesia's sustainable fishing zones**, help balance fishing needs with marine biodiversity conservation.

5. Economic Benefits – Livelihoods & Sustainable Tourism

Why It Matters:

- Coastal and marine industries contribute **$3 trillion to the global economy** annually.
- **Eco-tourism** provides jobs and revenue while promoting environmental conservation.

Example:

- **Whale-watching tourism** in places like Iceland and Canada generates millions in revenue while raising awareness about marine conservation.

- Sustainable fishing initiatives, like the **Marine Stewardship Council (MSC)**, ensure that fisheries remain profitable while protecting aquatic ecosystems.

6. Protection Against Natural Disasters

Why It Matters:

- Coral reefs and mangroves act as **natural barriers**, reducing the impact of tsunamis, hurricanes, and coastal erosion.
- Destruction of these ecosystems makes coastal communities more vulnerable to disasters.

Example:

- **Mangrove reforestation** in Bangladesh and the Philippines has helped protect coastal villages from storm surges and flooding.

7. Preventing Plastic Pollution & Toxic Contamination

Why It Matters:

- **Over 14 million tons of plastic** enter the ocean every year, harming marine life and ecosystems.
- Toxic chemicals from industrial waste contaminate drinking water sources.

Example:

- **The Ocean Cleanup Project** is removing plastic from the Great Pacific Garbage Patch.
- Countries banning **single-use plastics**, such as Canada and Kenya, reduce plastic waste entering rivers and oceans.

What Can We Do to Preserve Aquatic Life?

✓ **Reduce plastic waste** – Avoid single-use plastics and support recycling initiatives.

✓ **Support sustainable seafood** – Choose fish from responsibly managed sources.

✓ **Conserve water** – Reduce unnecessary water use to protect freshwater ecosystems.

✓ **Participate in community cleanups** – Help remove litter from local rivers, lakes, and beaches.

✓ **Protect marine habitats** – Support conservation organizations working to restore coral reefs and wetlands.

✓ **Advocate for policies** – Support laws that limit industrial pollution and overfishing.

Conclusion

Preserving aquatic life is not just about protecting marine species—it is about securing the **health of our planet and future generations**. By adopting sustainable habits and supporting conservation efforts, we can ensure that **oceans, rivers, and lakes**

remain thriving ecosystems that support biodiversity, climate stability, and human livelihoods.

✓ Restoration of Habitats – Rebuilding Natural Ecosystems

Why Habitat Restoration is Important?

Human activities such as **urbanization, deforestation, and pollution** have degraded natural habitats, leading to biodiversity loss. Restoring ecosystems **revives degraded lands and water bodies**, ensuring a sustainable future.

✓ **Rebuilds Natural Ecosystems** (Planet) – Restores forests, wetlands, and grasslands.

✓ **Mitigates Climate Change** (Prosperity) – Trees absorb carbon dioxide, reducing global warming.

✓ **Supports Local Communities** (People) – Restored habitats create jobs in conservation and ecotourism.

✓ **Encourages Collaboration** (Partnership) – Governments, NGOs, and corporations work together for restoration projects.

Habitat Restoration Methods

- **Reforestation & Afforestation** – Planting trees to restore forests.
- **Wetland Restoration** – Rebuilding marshes and swamps to absorb floods and filter water.
- **Soil Regeneration** – Using organic farming and regenerative agriculture to restore soil health.
- **Urban Greening Initiatives** – Creating green spaces, parks, and rooftop gardens in cities.
- **Protecting Pollinators** – Establishing bee-friendly habitats to enhance biodiversity.

Example: China's **Great Green Wall** project is planting **billions of trees** to stop desert expansion and restore ecosystems.

Example: Costa Rica's **Rainforest Regeneration Program** has restored over **50% of the country's deforested land** through reforestation efforts.

Example: The **United Nations Decade on Ecosystem Restoration (2021-2030)** aims to prevent, halt, and reverse environmental degradation worldwide.

Benefits of Restoration of Habitats – Rebuilding Natural Ecosystems

Restoring natural habitats is a **key pillar** of sustainability, essential for reversing environmental damage and supporting biodiversity, climate resilience, and human well-being. Ecosystem restoration involves rebuilding degraded forests, wetlands, grasslands, coral reefs, and other vital habitats to ensure long-term ecological balance.

✔ **Key Benefits of Habitat Restoration**

1. Restoring Biodiversity – Protecting Plants & Animals

Why It Matters:

- Healthy ecosystems **support diverse species**, preventing extinction and ensuring food chain stability.
- Restoring habitats helps **reintroduce endangered species** and improve breeding conditions for wildlife.

Example:

- The **Yellowstone National Park Wolf Reintroduction** (USA) restored predator-prey balance, increasing biodiversity.
- **India's Project Tiger** revived forests and grasslands, boosting the tiger population and restoring the ecosystem.

2. Improving Climate Resilience & Carbon Sequestration

Why It Matters:

- Restored habitats **absorb CO_2**, reducing global warming.
- Forests, wetlands, and mangroves **act as carbon sinks**, slowing climate change.

Example:

- The **Great Green Wall in Africa** is reforesting the Sahel region, reducing desertification and capturing carbon.
- **Mangrove restoration projects** in Bangladesh protect coastal communities from rising sea levels and extreme weather.

3. Enhancing Water Resources & Preventing Droughts

Why It Matters:

- Healthy wetlands and forests **regulate water cycles**, preventing floods and droughts.

- Restoring vegetation **improves groundwater recharge**, ensuring a reliable water supply.

Example:

- China's **Loess Plateau Restoration** reversed desertification, increasing water availability and restoring agriculture.
- **Wetland restoration in Canada's Prairie Pothole Region** improved water storage, reducing drought risks.

4. Boosting Agricultural Productivity & Food Security

Why It Matters:

- Restored ecosystems support **pollinators, soil fertility, and water retention**, improving farming yields.
- Agroforestry (planting trees in farmlands) **protects crops from climate extremes**.

Example:

- **Costa Rica's reforestation programs** have increased agricultural productivity and ecotourism.
- **Agroforestry in Kenya** has improved soil fertility and food production while reducing deforestation.

5. Preventing Natural Disasters – Floods, Landslides & Wildfires

Why It Matters:

- Trees and vegetation **stabilize soil**, preventing landslides.
- Wetlands and mangroves **act as natural barriers** against floods and storm surges.

Example:

- **New York City's wetland restoration** has reduced flood risks and improved water quality.
- **Indonesia's peatland restoration** has decreased wildfires and carbon emissions.

6. Strengthening Local & Indigenous Communities

Why It Matters:

- Restored habitats **provide sustainable livelihoods** (eco-tourism, fishing, farming).
- Indigenous communities **benefit from cultural and economic revival**.

Example:

- The **Amazon Rainforest Indigenous Restoration Projects** help protect biodiversity while supporting tribal communities.
- In **Australia, Indigenous fire management** has reduced wildfires and restored biodiversity.

7. Promoting Eco-Tourism & Economic Growth

Why It Matters:

- Rebuilt ecosystems attract **sustainable tourism**, creating jobs and boosting local economies.
- National parks, coral reefs, and rainforests generate revenue for conservation efforts.

Example:

- **Ecotourism in Rwanda's Volcanoes National Park** funds gorilla conservation and community development.

- Thailand's coral reef restoration has revived marine tourism while protecting biodiversity.

Mindsets that are required for this Sustainability Certification

1. Global Responsibility (UN SDG Alignment)

- Mindset: Understand that sustainability is a global effort, and individual actions contribute to achieving the UN Sustainable Development Goals (SDGs).

- **How to Build It:**

    - Learn the SDGs: Study the 17 UN SDGs and their relevance to your life.

    - Think Globally, Act Locally: Align your actions with global goals, such as reducing waste or conserving water.

    - Reflect: Regularly assess how your decisions impact global sustainability.

- **Behavior:**

    - Advocate for policies that align with the SDGs.

    - Support initiatives that address global challenges like poverty, inequality, and climate change.

2. Biodiversity Stewardship (Wildlife Conservation)

- Mindset: Recognize the intrinsic value of all species and their role in maintaining ecological balance.

- **How to Build It:**

    - Educate Yourself: Learn about endangered species and their habitats.

    - Connect with Nature: Spend time in natural environments to appreciate biodiversity.

- Advocate: Support conservation efforts and policies that protect wildlife.

- **Behavior:**

    - Avoid products made from endangered species (e.g., ivory, fur).

    - Support wildlife sanctuaries and conservation programs.

3. Aquatic Guardianship (Preserving Aquatic Life)

- Mindset: Treat oceans, rivers, and lakes as vital resources that must be protected.

- **How to Build It:**

    - Understand Water Ecosystems: Learn about the importance of aquatic life and the threats it faces.

    - Practice Conservation: Reduce plastic use, support sustainable fishing, and avoid polluting water bodies.

    - Innovate: Explore ways to reduce water pollution and restore aquatic habitats.

- **Behavior:**

    - Participate in beach or river cleanups.

    - Support marine protected areas and sustainable seafood initiatives.

4. Habitat Restoration (Rebuilding Ecosystems)

- Mindset: Take responsibility for restoring degraded environments to sustain biodiversity.

- **How to Build It:**

    - Learn About Ecosystems: Understand the importance of forests, wetlands, and grasslands.

- Get Involved: Participate in reforestation or wetland restoration projects.

    - Advocate: Push for policies that promote habitat restoration.

- **Behavior:**

    - Plant trees and support afforestation programs.

    - Volunteer for habitat restoration projects in your community.

How to Build These Mindsets

1. Education: Learn about sustainability principles and their real-world applications.

2. Practice: Start small—reduce waste, conserve water, and support conservation efforts.

3. Collaboration: Work with others to amplify your impact.

4. Reflection: Regularly assess your actions and their alignment with sustainability goals.

- Advocacy: Share your knowledge and inspire others to adopt sustainable practice

What Can We Do to Restore Habitats?

✓ **Plant native trees and vegetation** – Support reforestation and afforestation programs.

✓ **Protect existing forests and wetlands** – Avoid deforestation and land degradation.

✓ **Reduce pollution and waste** – Prevent toxins from harming natural ecosystems.

✓ **Support conservation organizations** – Volunteer or donate to habitat restoration initiatives.

✓ **Promote sustainable agriculture** – Encourage organic and regenerative farming practices.

✓ **Advocate for strong environmental policies** – Push for laws that protect natural habitats.

Conclusion:

Restoring habitats is not just about protecting wildlife and plants; it is about **securing the future of our planet**. Healthy ecosystems regulate the climate, provide clean water, and ensure food security. By taking action today, we can **rebuild natural ecosystems, restore balance, and create a more sustainable future** for all life on Earth.

CHAPTER 5

Orange HAT Certification (Intermediate - Level 2) - Sustainable Agriculture, Carbon Footprint Reduction Strategies, Soil and Land Conservation, Networking for Sustainability & Poverty Reduction

The **Orange HAT Certification** focuses on **practical sustainability solutions** that connect environmental responsibility with economic and social well-being. This certification helps individuals understand the importance of **sustainable agriculture, reducing carbon footprints, protecting land and soil, and networking for sustainability initiatives that also combat poverty**.

1. Sustainable Agriculture – Feeding the Future Responsibly

What is Sustainable Agriculture?

Sustainable agriculture refers to **farming methods that protect the environment, enhance soil fertility, conserve water, and reduce chemical dependency** while ensuring food security for future generations.

✔ **Benefits of Sustainable Agriculture:**

- **Reduces environmental impact** by minimizing deforestation and overgrazing.
- **Ensures long-term food security** through efficient land use.
- **Improves farmer income** by promoting organic and regenerative practices.
- **Reduces chemical pollution** and soil degradation.

Real-World Examples:

- **India's Zero Budget Natural Farming (ZBNF):** Farmers use bio-based fertilizers instead of chemicals, reducing costs and improving soil health.
- **Urban Rooftop Farming in Singapore:** Maximizes space for growing fresh produce while reducing food transportation emissions.
- **Agroforestry in Africa:** Growing trees alongside crops improves biodiversity, prevents soil erosion, and provides shade for crops.

2. Carbon Footprint Reduction Strategies – Cutting Down Emissions

What is a Carbon Footprint?

A **carbon footprint** is the total amount of **greenhouse gases (CO_2, methane, nitrous oxide, etc.)** produced by human activities, industries, and daily consumption habits.

Benefits of Reducing Carbon Footprints:

- **Mitigates climate change** by cutting global emissions.
- **Improves air quality** and public health.
- **Enhances energy efficiency**, saving resources and costs.

Real-World Examples:

- **Renewable Energy in Iceland:** 100% of electricity comes from renewable sources (hydropower and geothermal).
- **Electric Vehicles (EVs) in Norway:** Over 80% of new cars sold are EVs, reducing fossil fuel dependency.
- **Sustainable Diets:** The shift toward plant-based eating in Europe has significantly reduced methane emissions from livestock.

How Individuals Can Reduce Their Carbon Footprint:

✓ Use **public transportation, cycling, or electric vehicles.**

✓ Switch to **solar panels** and **energy-efficient appliances.**

✓ Reduce **meat consumption** and buy **locally sourced food.**

✓ Implement **waste management** by composting and recycling.

3. Soil & Land Conservation – Protecting Our Foundation

Why is Soil Conservation Important?

Soil is **the foundation of agriculture** and essential for maintaining food security. However, soil degradation due to **deforestation, excessive chemical use, and urbanization** threatens future generations.

Benefits of Soil & Land Conservation:

- **Prevents desertification** and land degradation.
- **Enhances agricultural productivity** by maintaining fertile soil.
- **Reduces floods and landslides** through better land management.
- **Preserves biodiversity** by protecting natural habitats.

Real-World Examples:

- **The Great Green Wall (Africa):** A 7,000 km tree-planting initiative across the Sahara Desert to combat desertification.
- **Terrace Farming in the Philippines:** Reduces soil erosion while maximizing land use for agriculture.

- **Biochar Farming in South America:** Enhances soil fertility by locking carbon into the ground.

Ways to Conserve Soil & Land:

✓ **No-till farming** – Reduces soil erosion.
✓ **Crop rotation & cover crops** – Maintains soil nutrients.
✓ **Reforestation efforts** – Restores degraded land.
✓ **Organic composting** – Improves soil health.

4. Networking for Sustainability & Poverty Reduction – Collective Action

Why is Networking Important for Sustainability?

Sustainability challenges require **collaborative solutions**. By **connecting individuals, organizations, and governments**, we can amplify impact, share best practices, and drive large-scale change.

Benefits of Networking for Sustainability:

- **Encourages knowledge sharing** and innovation.
- **Attracts investment** in sustainable businesses and projects.
- **Strengthens community resilience** against environmental and economic challenges.
- **Creates employment opportunities**, reducing poverty.

Real-World Examples:

- **Fair Trade Certification:** Helps small farmers in developing countries sell products at fair prices while promoting sustainable agriculture.
- **Women's Cooperatives in Bangladesh:** Groups like the Grameen Bank empower women to start small eco-friendly businesses, reducing poverty.
- **Sustainable Development Goals (SDG) Partnerships:** UN-led initiatives bring together governments, NGOs, and businesses to tackle poverty and environmental challenges.

✓ Ways to Get Involved in Sustainability Networking:

✓ Join environmental and social impact organizations.

✓ Support local farmers' markets and ethical brands.

✓ Participate in community-driven sustainability projects.

✓ Leverage technology to connect with global sustainability initiatives.

Mindsets that are required for this Sustainability Certification:

1. Responsible Farming (Sustainable Agriculture)

- Mindset: Recognize that farming practices must balance productivity with environmental stewardship.
- **How to Build It:**
    - Educate Yourself: Learn about sustainable farming methods like crop rotation, organic farming, and agroforestry.
    - Support Local Farmers: Buy from farmers who use sustainable practices.
    - Advocate: Promote policies that support sustainable agriculture.
- **Behavior:**
    - Grow your own food using sustainable methods.
    - Support organic and regenerative farming initiatives.

2. Climate Consciousness (Carbon Footprint Reduction)

- Mindset: Understand the impact of your actions on the climate and take responsibility for reducing emissions.

- **How to Build It:**
    - Learn About Carbon Footprints: Understand how daily activities contribute to greenhouse gas emissionsAdopt Green Habits: Use public transport, switch to renewable energy, and reduce meat consumption.

    - Innovate: Explore ways to reduce energy use and waste in your home and workplace.

- **Behavior:**

    - Use energy-efficient appliances and renewable energy sources.

    - Reduce, reuse, and recycle to minimize waste.

3. Land Stewardship (Soil and Land Conservation)

- Mindset: Treat soil and land as precious resources that must be protected and restored.

- **How to Build It:**

    - Understand Soil Health: Learn about the importance of soil fertility and the threats it faces.

    - Practice Conservation: Use no-till farming, crop rotation, and organic composting.

    - Advocate: Support policies that protect land and promote reforestation.

- **Behavior:**

    - Plant trees and support afforestation programs.

    - Participate in soil conservation projects.

4. Collaborative Action (Networking for Sustainability)

- Mindset: Recognize that sustainability challenges require collective solutions.

- **How to Build It:**

    - Build Networks: Connect with like-minded individuals and organizations.

    - Share Resources: Pool resources for community projects like urban gardens.

    - Celebrate Collective Wins: Recognize group achievements in sustainability.

- **Behavior:**

    - Join or start a community sustainability project.

    - Share knowledge and tools with others

Conclusion – The Power of the Orange HAT Certification

The **Orange HAT Certification** focuses on **intermediate-level sustainability actions** that balance **environmental conservation, social responsibility, and economic progress**. By mastering these skills, individuals become **active sustainability practitioners** who help create a **greener, more equitable world**.

✓ **Sustainable Agriculture** protects natural resources and ensures food security.
✓ **Carbon Footprint Reduction Strategies** lower greenhouse gas emissions.
✓ **Soil & Land Conservation** safeguards agricultural productivity and biodiversity.
✓ **Networking for Sustainability & Poverty Reduction** fosters economic empowerment and resilience.

CHAPTER 6

Red HAT Certification (Intermediate - Level 2) - Leadership: Organizing Sustainability Campaigns, Leadership for Environmental Action, Goal Setting and Vision Making, Individual Sustainability Mindset Measures

The Red HAT Certification is designed to develop leaders who can inspire and organize sustainability efforts in their communities and workplaces. This certification equips individuals with skills in organizing sustainability campaigns, leading environmental action, setting goals for a sustainable future, and cultivating a personal sustainability mindset.

Key Focus Areas:

✓ Organizing Sustainability Campaigns – Mobilizing people for action.

✓ Leadership for Environmental Action – Becoming an effective sustainability advocate.

✓ Goal Setting & Vision Making – Creating long-term sustainability plans.

✓ Individual Sustainability Mindset Measures – Tracking and improving sustainable habits.

1. Organizing Sustainability Campaigns – Mobilizing People for Impact

What is a Sustainability Campaign?

A sustainability campaign is an organized effort to raise awareness and drive action toward environmental and social issues. These campaigns can focus on climate change, waste reduction, energy efficiency, water conservation, biodiversity protection, and social equity.

Benefits of Organizing Sustainability Campaigns:

- Increases awareness and education about sustainability issues.
- Encourages community participation in environmental efforts.
- Drives real-world action such as tree planting, cleanups, or policy changes.
- Builds leadership and teamwork skills among participants.

Real-World Examples:

- Earth Hour (Global): Encourages people to turn off non-essential lights for one hour to raise awareness about energy conservation.
- Plastic-Free July (Global): Challenges individuals to reduce plastic consumption.
- Mission LiFE (India): Promotes sustainable lifestyles by encouraging individual and community action.
- Adopt-a-Beach (USA): Volunteers clean up beaches to prevent ocean pollution.

Steps to Organize a Sustainability Campaign:

✓ Identify an issue (e.g., plastic waste, deforestation, air pollution).

✓ Define a goal (e.g., reduce single-use plastic in your city by 50%).

✓ Build a team and partnerships to increase impact.

✓ Use social media, local events, and influencers for outreach.

✓ Take measurable actions (e.g., collect 10,000 kg of waste, plant 5,000 trees).

✓ Track progress and results to inspire more people.

2. Leadership for Environmental Action – Becoming a Sustainability Advocate

What is Sustainability Leadership?

Sustainability leaders influence and inspire people to take action for the planet. They promote eco-friendly policies, ethical business practices, and community-driven sustainability projects.

Benefits of Leadership in Sustainability:

- Influences positive change in policies, organizations, and communities.
- Creates long-term environmental and social impact.
- Builds skills in communication, teamwork, and strategic thinking.
- Encourages a culture of responsibility and sustainable habits.

Real-World Examples:

- Greta Thunberg (Sweden): Inspired millions through climate strikes and advocacy.
- Wangari Maathai (Kenya): Founded the Green Belt Movement, planting over 50 million trees.
- Boyan Slat (Netherlands): Developed The Ocean Cleanup project to remove plastic from oceans.
- Vanessa Nakate (Uganda): Advocates for climate justice in Africa.

How to Develop Leadership for Environmental Action:

✓ Educate yourself about sustainability issues.

✓ Lead by example (practice what you preach).

✓ Inspire and engage your community.

✓ Collaborate with organizations, businesses, and governments.

✓ Advocate for policy changes and sustainable business models.

3. Goal Setting & Vision Making – Creating a Roadmap for Sustainability

Why is Goal Setting Important in Sustainability?

Sustainability requires long-term vision and well-defined goals. Without clear objectives, efforts can become disorganized and ineffective.

Benefits of Setting Sustainability Goals:

- Provides direction and focus for sustainability efforts.
- Ensures measurable impact by tracking progress.
- Encourages accountability in businesses, governments, and individuals.
- Helps integrate sustainability into personal and professional life.

Real-World Examples:

- United Nations Sustainable Development Goals (SDGs): 17 global goals to end poverty, protect the planet, and ensure prosperity by 2030.
- India's Net-Zero Target: India aims to achieve net-zero emissions by 2070.
- Amazon's Climate Pledge: Amazon aims to be carbon-neutral by 2040.
- Tesla's Vision for Clean Energy: Focuses on electric vehicles and renewable energy solutions.

Steps to Set Sustainability Goals:

✓ Identify key sustainability areas (waste reduction, energy efficiency, biodiversity).
✓ Use the SMART approach (Specific, Measurable, Achievable, Relevant, Time-bound).
✓ Break down long-term goals into short-term milestones.
✓ Continuously track progress and adjust strategies.

4. Individual Sustainability Mindset Measures – Personal Accountability

What is an Individual Sustainability Mindset?

A sustainability mindset means making eco-conscious decisions in everyday life, from the products you buy to how you use resources.

Benefits of an Individual Sustainability Mindset:

- Reduces environmental footprint at a personal level.
- Promotes healthier and more ethical lifestyles.
- Encourages mindful consumption and responsible decision-making.
- Influences families, workplaces, and communities to adopt sustainable practices.

Real-World Examples:

- Minimalist Lifestyle: Buying less and prioritizing needs over wants.
- Meatless Mondays: Reducing meat consumption to lower carbon footprints.
- Zero-Waste Living: Avoiding plastic and disposable products.
- Eco-Friendly Homes: Using solar energy, water-saving devices, and sustainable materials.

How to Cultivate a Sustainability Mindset:

✓ Track your carbon footprint and make lifestyle changes.
✓ Follow the 5Rs: Refuse, Reduce, Reuse, Recycle, Rot.
✓ Buy from ethical and sustainable brands.
✓ Support local and fair-trade products.
✓ Choose public transport, cycling, or walking whenever possible.

Mindsets that are required for this Sustainability Certification

1. Mobilization Mindset (Organizing Sustainability Campaigns)

- Mindset: Believe in the power of collective action to drive change.

- **How to Build It:**

  - Educate Yourself: Learn about successful campaigns like Earth Hour or Plastic-Free July.

  - Start Small: Organize a local cleanup or tree-planting event.

  - Collaborate: Build partnerships with local organizations, schools, and businesses.

- **Behavior:**

  - Identify a sustainability issue and set a clear goal.

  - Use social media and community events to mobilize people.

  - Measure and share the impact of your campaign.

2. Advocacy Mindset (Leadership for Environmental Action)

- Mindset: Understand that leadership is about inspiring and influencing others.

- **How to Build It:**

  - Lead by Example: Practice sustainable habits in your daily life.

  - Educate Others: Share knowledge about sustainability issues and solutions.

  - Advocate: Push for policies and practices that promote sustainability.

- **Behavior:**

  - Speak at community events or schools about sustainability.

  - Collaborate with organizations to amplify your impact.

  - Advocate for policy changes that support environmental action.

3. Visionary Mindset (Goal Setting & Vision Making)

- Mindset: Think long-term and set clear, actionable goals for sustainability.

- **How to Build It:**

  - Learn from Examples: Study global goals like the UN SDGs or corporate sustainability pledges.

  - Set SMART Goals: Make goals Specific, Measurable, Achievable, Relevant, and Time-bound.

  - Track Progress: Regularly assess and adjust your strategies.

- **Behavior:**

  - Create a personal or organizational sustainability roadmap.

  - Break down long-term goals into short-term milestones.

  - Celebrate achievements to stay motivated.

4. Accountability Mindset (Individual Sustainability Mindset Measures)

- Mindset: Take personal responsibility for your environmental impact.

- **How to Build It:**

  - Track Your Footprint: Use tools to measure your carbon footprint.

  - Adopt the 5Rs: Refuse, Reduce, Reuse, Recycle, Rot.

  - Reflect: Regularly assess your habits and make improvements.

- **Behavior:**

  - Reduce waste by avoiding single-use plastics.

  - Choose sustainable products and support ethical brands.

  - Use public transport, cycling, or walking to reduce emissions.

Conclusion – The Power of the Red HAT Certification

The Red HAT Certification is designed for individuals who want to lead sustainability efforts in their organizations, communities, and personal lives. It teaches practical leadership skills, campaign strategies, goal setting, and self-discipline in adopting a sustainable mindset.

✓ Organizing Sustainability Campaigns builds awareness and mobilizes action.
✓ Leadership for Environmental Action inspires and influences change.
✓ Goal Setting & Vision Making ensures sustainability is a long-term priority.
✓ Individual Sustainability Mindset Measures create personal responsibility.

CHAPTER 7

Purple Hat Certification (Intermediate - Level 2) - Sustainable Packaging, Consumer Responsibility In Sustainability, Smart Cities, Innovation In Circular Economy

The purple hat certification is designed for individuals who want to explore sustainable packaging, consumer responsibility, smart cities, and innovation in the circular economy. This level focuses on how businesses, consumers, and governments can work together to reduce waste, improve urban sustainability, and create innovative solutions for a greener planet.

Key Focus Areas:

✓ Sustainable Packaging – Reducing environmental impact through eco-friendly materials.
✓ Consumer Responsibility in Sustainability – Encouraging mindful consumption.
✓ Smart Cities – Using technology and sustainability practices to improve urban living.
✓ Innovation in the Circular Economy – Finding creative ways to reuse and recycle resources.

1. Sustainable Packaging – Reducing Environmental Impact

What is Sustainable Packaging?

Sustainable packaging refers to materials and designs that minimize waste and reduce carbon footprint. This includes biodegradable materials, recyclable packaging, reusable designs, and minimalist approaches that use fewer resources.

Benefits of Sustainable Packaging:

- Reduces plastic pollution and landfill waste.
- Decreases carbon emissions from production and transportation.
- Encourages consumers to make eco-friendly choices.
- Saves costs for businesses by using sustainable alternatives.

Real-World Examples:

- Unilever's Refillable Packaging: Offers refill stations for shampoo and detergent.
- Coca-Cola's Plant Bottle: Uses plant-based plastic to reduce fossil fuel dependency.
- Nike's Shoe Boxes: Made from recycled cardboard with soy-based ink.
- Amazon's Frustration-Free Packaging: Uses 100% recyclable materials with minimal waste.

How to Implement Sustainable Packaging:

✓ Use compostable or biodegradable materials (e.g., cornstarch-based plastics, bamboo).

✓ Encourage refillable and reusable packaging (e.g., glass bottles, stainless steel containers).

✓ Design minimalist packaging to reduce excess material use.

✓ Choose recyclable and FSC-certified paper for packaging.

2. Consumer Responsibility in Sustainability – Making Mindful Choices

What is Consumer Responsibility?

Consumers play a crucial role in sustainability by choosing products that are ethical, eco-friendly, and support responsible businesses. Every purchase has an impact on deforestation, carbon emissions, pollution, and waste.

Benefits of Consumer Responsibility:

- Reduces environmental damage by supporting green businesses.
- Encourages companies to adopt sustainable practices.
- Promotes ethical labor and fair trade policies.
- Reduces waste through conscious purchasing habits.

Real-World Examples:

- Fair Trade Coffee & Chocolate: Consumers choose brands that ensure ethical labor and sustainable farming.
- Fast Fashion vs. Slow Fashion: People opt for sustainable clothing brands like Patagonia instead of fast fashion brands that exploit workers and the environment.
- Meat Consumption Reduction: Consumers choose plant-based or ethically sourced meat to lower their carbon footprint.

How to Be a Responsible Consumer:

✓ Buy from ethical and sustainable brands.

✓ Reduce single-use plastic consumption.

✓ Support local and fair-trade products.

✓ Choose durable and long-lasting goods over cheap, disposable ones.

3. Smart Cities – Sustainable Urban Living

What are Smart Cities?

Smart cities use technology, data, and sustainable infrastructure to improve urban life while reducing environmental impact. These cities prioritize clean energy, efficient transportation, green spaces, and waste management solutions.

Benefits of Smart Cities:

- Reduces traffic congestion with smart transportation systems.
- Lowers carbon footprint with renewable energy sources.
- Improves air quality with green spaces and pollution monitoring.
- Enhances waste management with AI-based recycling programs.

Real-World Examples:

- Singapore's Smart Nation Program: Uses AI and IoT for smart traffic control, energy efficiency, and urban planning.
- Copenhagen's Bicycle Infrastructure: Over 50% of residents commute by bicycle, reducing CO2 emissions.
- Masdar City, UAE: A planned city that runs entirely on renewable energy.
- Barcelona's Smart Waste Bins: Uses sensors to optimize waste collection routes.

How to Contribute to Smart Cities:

✓ Support public transport and cycling infrastructure.
✓ Advocate for renewable energy policies in cities.
✓ Participate in community-driven urban sustainability projects.
✓ Use smart home technologies to reduce energy consumption.

4. Innovation in the Circular Economy – Creating Zero-Waste Solutions

What is the Circular Economy?

The circular economy focuses on reusing, refurbishing, remanufacturing, and recycling materials instead of disposing of them. This system eliminates waste and keeps resources in use for as long as possible.

Benefits of the Circular Economy:

- Reduces waste and pollution.
- Encourages sustainable business models.
- Saves costs by maximizing resource use.
- Promotes economic growth through green industries.

Real-World Examples:

- IKEA's Buy-Back Program: Allows customers to return old furniture for resale or recycling.
- Adidas' Futurecraft Loop Sneakers: 100% recyclable shoes that can be remade into new ones.
- Loop by Teracycle: A global initiative where brands like Unilever and Nestlé offer reusable packaging.
- Dell's Closed-Loop Recycling: Uses old electronics to manufacture new ones.

How to Promote the Circular Economy:

✓ Choose products made from recycled materials.

✓ Repair and reuse items instead of throwing them away.

✓ Support companies with take-back and recycling programs.

✓ Advocate for government policies that promote circular economies.

Mindsets that are required for this Sustainability Certification:

1. Eco-Innovation Mindset (Sustainable Packaging)
- **Mindset:** Believe in the power of innovation to reduce waste and environmental impact.

- **How to Build It:**
    - **Educate Yourself:** Learn about sustainable materials like biodegradable plastics and recycled paper.
    - **Experiment:** Try new packaging designs that minimize waste.
    - **Collaborate:** Work with suppliers and designers to create eco-friendly solutions.

- **Behavior:**
  - Use compostable or biodegradable materials for packaging.
  - Design minimalist packaging to reduce excess material use.
  - Advocate for recyclable and FSC-certified paper.

2. Conscious Consumer Mindset (Consumer Responsibility)

- **Mindset:** Understand that every purchase has an environmental and social impact.

- **How to Build It:**
  - **Educate Yourself:** Learn about the environmental impact of different products.
  - **Make Informed Choices:** Choose products that are ethical, eco-friendly, and support responsible businesses.
  - **Advocate:** Encourage others to make mindful purchasing decisions.
- **Behavior:**
  - Buy from ethical and sustainable brands.
  - Reduce single-use plastic consumption.
  - Support local and fair-trade products.

3. Urban Stewardship Mindset (Smart Cities)

- **Mindset:** Recognize the importance of sustainable urban living and the role of technology in achieving it.
- **How to Build It:**
  - **Educate Yourself:** Learn about smart city technologies and their benefits.
  - **Participate:** Get involved in community-driven urban sustainability projects.
  - **Advocate:** Push for policies that promote renewable energy and efficient transportation.
- **Behavior:**
  - Support public transport and cycling infrastructure.
  - Use smart home technologies to reduce energy consumption.
  - Advocate for renewable energy policies in cities.

4. Circular Thinking Mindset (Innovation in Circular Economy)

- **Mindset:** Believe in the power of reusing, refurbishing, and recycling to eliminate waste.
- **How to Build It:**
  - **Educate Yourself:** Learn about the principles of the circular economy.
  - **Experiment:** Try new ways to reuse and recycle materials.
  - **Collaborate:** Work with businesses and communities to promote circular practices.
- **Behavior:**
  - Choose products made from recycled materials.
  - Repair and reuse items instead of throwing them away.
  - Support companies with take-back and recycling programs.

Conclusion – The Power of the Purple HAT Certification

The Purple HAT Certification is for individuals who want to lead sustainability efforts in business, urban development, and consumer responsibility. It focuses on sustainable packaging, conscious consumption, smart city development, and circular economy innovations to build a greener future.

✓ Sustainable Packaging reduces pollution and waste.

✓ Consumer Responsibility empowers individuals to make sustainable choices.

✓ Smart Cities use technology to create eco-friendly urban environments.

✓ Innovation in the Circular Economy eliminates waste through creative solutions.

Brown HAT Certification (Intermediate - Level 2) - Environmental Policies, Circular Economy Models, Sustainable Tourism Policies, Green Finance & Ethical Corporate Governance

The **Brown HAT Certification** focuses on the **policy and governance aspects of sustainability**, equipping individuals with knowledge of **environmental regulations, circular economy models, sustainable tourism, and green finance**. It is designed for professionals, policymakers, and sustainability advocates who aim to **influence decision-making at governmental, corporate, and community levels**.

Key Focus Areas:

✓ **Environmental Policies** – Laws and regulations for sustainable development.
✓ **Circular Economy Models** – Creating zero-waste systems for long-term sustainability.
✓ **Sustainable Tourism Policies** – Balancing economic growth with environmental protection.
✓ **Green Finance & Ethical Corporate Governance** – Funding and business ethics for sustainability.

1. Environmental Policies – Laws & Regulations for a Greener Future

What are Environmental Policies?

Environmental policies are **rules, laws, and regulations** that protect the planet by **reducing pollution, conserving biodiversity, and promoting sustainability**. Governments, businesses, and organizations **enforce these policies** to address climate change, waste management, and resource conservation.

Benefits of Environmental Policies:

- **Reduces pollution and promotes cleaner air and water.**
- **Encourages businesses to adopt eco-friendly practices.**
- **Protects endangered species and ecosystems.**
- **Creates green jobs and sustainable industries.**

Real-World Examples:

- **Paris Climate Agreement (2015):** A global treaty to reduce carbon emissions and slow climate change.
- **Plastic Ban in India (2022):** Single-use plastics were banned to reduce pollution.
- **Carbon Tax in Sweden:** Companies pay a tax based on their carbon emissions, encouraging green energy.

- **Extended Producer Responsibility (EPR) in the EU:** Companies must manage waste disposal for their products.

How to Support Environmental Policies:

✓ Advocate for stronger **climate laws and carbon pricing.**

✓ Support **renewable energy incentives and pollution controls.**

✓ Push for **corporate responsibility in environmental impact.**

✓ Educate communities on **policy benefits and compliance.**

2. Circular Economy Models – Sustainable Resource Management

What is a Circular Economy?

A circular economy replaces the traditional **"take, make, dispose"** model with a **"reduce, reuse, recycle"** approach. It **minimizes waste, conserves resources, and extends product life cycles.**

Benefits of Circular Economy Models:

- **Reduces waste and pollution.**
- **Lowers carbon footprint by reusing materials.**
- **Encourages businesses to develop sustainable products.**
- **Creates new jobs in recycling, repair, and remanufacturing.**

Real-World Examples:

- **Patagonia's Worn Wear Program:** Customers can return old clothes for repair and resale.
- **IKEA's Circular Hub:** Encourages customers to return used furniture for refurbishment.
- **Philips' Lighting as a Service:** Instead of selling bulbs, Philips provides light as a service, reducing waste.
- **Ellen MacArthur Foundation:** Works with businesses to implement circular economy principles.

How to Implement a Circular Economy:

✓ Support **recycling and upcycling programs**.

✓ Choose **repairable and durable products**.

✓ Advocate for **businesses to adopt take-back programs**.

✓ Reduce **single-use products** and prefer **circular design**.

3. Sustainable Tourism Policies – Preserving Destinations for Future Generations

What is Sustainable Tourism?

Sustainable tourism ensures that travel does not **harm local communities, wildlife, or ecosystems**. It focuses on **eco-friendly travel, cultural preservation, and economic benefits for local populations**.

Benefits of Sustainable Tourism:

- Protects natural habitats and biodiversity.
- Supports local economies and cultures.
- Reduces pollution and over-tourism damage.
- Encourages responsible travel behavior.

Real-World Examples:

- **Bhutan's High-Value, Low-Impact Tourism Policy:** Limits visitor numbers and charges a sustainability fee.
- **Costa Rica's Ecotourism Model:** Promotes eco-lodges and wildlife conservation.
- **Palau's Responsible Tourism Law:** Visitors sign a pledge to protect the environment.
- **Amsterdam's Sustainable Tourism Strategy:** Encourages off-peak travel and cultural experiences.

How to Support Sustainable Tourism:

✓ Choose **eco-friendly hotels and travel operators**.

✓ Respect **local cultures and natural environments**.

✓ Reduce **waste while traveling** (carry reusable bottles and bags).

✓ Support **community-based tourism** that benefits locals.

4. Green Finance & Ethical Corporate Governance – Investing in Sustainability

What is Green Finance?

Green finance refers to **investments that support environmental sustainability**, including **renewable energy projects, sustainable businesses, and eco-friendly infrastructure**.

Benefits of Green Finance:

- Funds renewable energy and climate solutions.
- Encourages businesses to adopt sustainable practices.
- Reduces risks of environmental disasters.
- Increases transparency and ethical business practices.

Real-World Examples:

- **Green Bonds (World Bank & Apple):** Companies issue bonds to finance renewable energy projects.
- **Tesla's Sustainable Investments:** Focuses on electric vehicles and solar energy.
- **European Green Deal:** Aims to make Europe carbon-neutral by 2050.
- **Corporate ESG Reporting (Microsoft, Google):** Tracks sustainability progress in businesses.

What is Ethical Corporate Governance?

Ethical corporate governance ensures that companies **operate transparently, responsibly, and in alignment with sustainability goals**. This includes **fair labor policies, reducing environmental harm, and making long-term responsible business decisions**.

Benefits of Ethical Corporate Governance:

- Prevents corruption and corporate fraud.
- Encourages sustainability leadership in businesses.
- Attracts responsible investors and customers.
- Reduces risks of environmental damage and scandals.

Real-World Examples:

- **Unilever's Sustainable Living Plan:** Integrates sustainability into corporate strategy.
- **Patagonia's Ethical Business Model:** Donates profits to environmental causes.
- **Walmart's Renewable Energy Commitment:** Targets 100% renewable energy by 2040.
- **Starbucks' Ethical Sourcing Policy:** Ensures fair wages and sustainable coffee production.

✓ **How to Promote Green Finance & Ethical Governance:**

✓ Invest in **sustainable funds and green bonds**.

✓ Support **companies with strong ESG policies**.

✓ Demand **corporate transparency on sustainability issues**.

✓ Encourage **businesses to adopt ethical labor and environmental policies**.

Mindsets That are required for this Sustainability Certification:

1. Policy Advocacy Mindset (Environmental Policies)
- **Mindset:** Believe in the power of laws and regulations to drive environmental change.

- **How to Build It:**
  - **Educate Yourself:** Learn about global and local environmental policies like the Paris Agreement or carbon taxes.
  - **Advocate:** Push for stronger climate laws and corporate accountability.
  - **Collaborate:** Work with governments, NGOs, and businesses to implement policies.
- **Behavior:**
  - Support renewable energy incentives and pollution controls.
  - Advocate for Extended Producer Responsibility (EPR) and carbon pricing.
  - Educate communities on the benefits of environmental policies.

2. Circular Thinking Mindset (Circular Economy Models)
- **Mindset:** Embrace the idea of reusing, refurbishing, and recycling to eliminate waste.
- **How to Build It:**
  - **Learn the Principles:** Study circular economy models like Patagonia's Worn Wear or IKEA's Circular Hub.
  - **Experiment:** Try new ways to reuse and recycle materials in your personal or professional life.
  - **Collaborate:** Work with businesses and communities to promote circular practices.
- **Behavior:**
  - Support recycling and upcycling programs.
  - Choose repairable and durable products.
  - Advocate for businesses to adopt take-back programs.

3. Responsible Tourism Mindset (Sustainable Tourism Policies)

- **Mindset:** Recognize the importance of balancing tourism with environmental and cultural preservation.
- **How to Build It:**
    - **Educate Yourself:** Learn about sustainable tourism models like Bhutan's High-Value, Low-Impact policy.
    - **Practice:** Choose eco-friendly travel options and respect local cultures.
    - **Advocate:** Push for policies that promote sustainable tourism.

- **Behavior:**
    - Support eco-friendly hotels and travel operators.
    - Reduce waste while traveling (e.g., carry reusable bottles and bags).
    - Advocate for community-based tourism that benefits locals.

4. Ethical Investment Mindset (Green Finance & Ethical Corporate Governance)

- **Mindset:** Understand that financial decisions can drive sustainability and ethical practices.
- **How to Build It:**
    - **Educate Yourself:** Learn about green finance tools like green bonds and ESG reporting.
    - **Invest Responsibly:** Choose sustainable funds and support companies with strong ESG policies.
    - **Advocate:** Push for corporate transparency and ethical governance.
    -

- **Behavior:**
    - Invest in sustainable funds and green bonds.
    - Support companies with strong ESG policies.

Demand corporate transparency on sustainability issues

Conclusion – The Power of the Brown HAT Certification

The **Brown HAT Certification** empowers individuals to **drive policy and financial decisions that support sustainability**. It is ideal for those working in **government, corporate leadership, finance, and tourism**, as well as sustainability advocates seeking **systemic change**.

✓ Environmental Policies ensure sustainable regulations and enforcement.
✓ Circular Economy Models eliminate waste and maximize resource use.
✓ Sustainable Tourism Policies balance economic benefits with environmental protection.
✓ Green Finance & Ethical Corporate Governance guide responsible investments and business practices.

CHAPTER 9

Grey Hat Certification (Advanced - Level 3) - Self-Awareness, Crisis Management In Climate Change, Global Climate Resilience Strategies, Deforestation, Role Of Esg In Decision-Making

The grey hat certification is an advanced-level certification within the Zha sustainability mindset framework. It focuses on self-awareness, crisis management in climate change, global climate resilience strategies, deforestation, and the role of ESG (environmental, social, and governance) in decision-making. This certification is designed for leaders, policymakers, corporate executives, and sustainability professionals who want to drive climate action, resilience planning, and responsible governance.

Key Focus Areas:

✓ Self-Awareness – Understanding personal impact on the environment.
✓ Crisis Management in Climate Change – Responding to extreme climate events.
✓ Global Climate Resilience Strategies – Preparing for climate challenges.

✓ Deforestation – Addressing and preventing forest loss.
✓ Role of ESG in Decision-Making – Integrating sustainability in business and governance.

1. Self-Awareness – Understanding Your Role in Sustainability

What is Self-Awareness in Sustainability?

Self-awareness means recognizing how personal choices impact the environment and society. It includes conscious decision-making in energy use, waste management, water conservation, and consumer behavior.

Benefits of Self-Awareness in Sustainability:

- Encourages responsible consumption and waste reduction.
- Promotes ethical choices in food, clothing, and transportation.
- Inspires others to adopt a sustainable lifestyle.
- Reduces individual carbon footprint.

Real-World Examples:

- Minimalist Living: People reducing unnecessary consumption to lower waste.
- Meatless Mondays: Reducing meat consumption to decrease carbon emissions.
- Slow Fashion Movement: Choosing sustainable clothing brands over fast fashion.
- Personal Carbon Footprint Tracking Apps (e.g., Earth Hero, Klima): Help individuals track and reduce emissions.

How to Practice Self-Awareness:

✓ Track daily resource usage (electricity, water, fuel, food waste).
✓ Choose eco-friendly products and brands.
✓ Support sustainable companies and policies.
✓ Educate yourself and others on sustainability issues.

2. Crisis Management in Climate Change – Responding to Extreme Events

What is Climate Crisis Management?

Crisis management in climate change involves preparing for, responding to, and recovering from natural disasters and extreme weather events caused by global warming, such as floods, hurricanes, droughts, and wildfires.

Benefits of Climate Crisis Management:

- Saves lives and reduces economic damage.
- Enhances community resilience and disaster preparedness.
- Protects critical infrastructure and ecosystems.
- Reduces long-term recovery costs.

Real-World Examples:

- Early Warning Systems (Bangladesh): Cyclone preparedness reduced deaths from thousands to dozens.
- Netherlands' Flood Management: Uses advanced water barriers and smart dikes to prevent flooding.
- California Wildfire Prevention: Controlled burns and stricter regulations to prevent large-scale fires.
- Urban Heat Management (Singapore's Green Plan 2030): Increased green cover to combat rising temperatures.

How to Implement Climate Crisis Management:

✓ Support disaster risk reduction policies.

✓ Develop emergency response plans for communities.

✓ Invest in climate-resilient infrastructure.

✓ Educate people on climate emergency preparedness.

3. Global Climate Resilience Strategies – Building a Sustainable Future

What is Climate Resilience?

Climate resilience refers to the ability of communities, ecosystems, and economies to adapt to and recover from climate-related disruptions. It focuses on reducing vulnerabilities and ensuring long-term sustainability.

Benefits of Climate Resilience Strategies:

- Protects vulnerable populations from climate shocks.
- Promotes sustainable agriculture and food security.
- Encourages renewable energy and water conservation.
- Ensures cities and businesses adapt to future climate risks.

Real-World Examples:

- Green Roofs in New York City: Reduces urban heat islands and improves air quality.
- Mangrove Restoration (Indonesia): Protects coastlines from rising sea levels.
- Water Recycling in Israel: Advanced irrigation techniques reduce water scarcity.
- Africa's Great Green Wall: Planting trees to combat desertification in the Sahel region.

How to Strengthen Climate Resilience:

✓ Support reforestation and ecosystem restoration projects.
✓ Invest in green infrastructure and water conservation.
✓ Encourage climate adaptation policies at local and national levels.
✓ Promote community-driven sustainability initiatives.

4. Deforestation – The Urgent Need for Forest Conservation

What is Deforestation?

Deforestation is the destruction of forests for agriculture, urbanization, and logging, leading to biodiversity loss, increased carbon emissions, and climate instability.

Benefits of Preventing Deforestation:

- Preserves biodiversity and endangered species.
- Reduces carbon emissions and combats climate change.
- Protects indigenous communities and local economies.
- Maintains water cycles and prevents soil erosion.

Real-World Examples:

- Amazon Rainforest Conservation Efforts: Brazil enforces stricter deforestation laws.
- REDD+ Program (UN Initiative): Financial incentives for countries to protect forests.
- Eden Reforestation Projects (Africa & Asia): Provides jobs while restoring forests.
- Norway's Zero Deforestation Policy: Country refuses to import deforestation-linked products.

How to Prevent Deforestation:

✓ Support reforestation programs and tree-planting initiatives.

✓ Reduce paper and wood consumption.

✓ Boycott products linked to illegal deforestation (e.g., palm oil, unsustainable beef).

✓ Advocate for stricter forest conservation policies.

5. Role of ESG (Environmental, Social, and Governance) in Decision-Making

What is ESG?

ESG stands for Environmental, Social, and Governance, a framework that guides companies to make ethical, sustainable, and responsible business decisions.

Benefits of ESG in Decision-Making:

- Encourages ethical corporate responsibility.
- Reduces environmental damage from industries.
- Increases transparency and accountability.
- Attracts sustainable investments and ethical consumers.

Real-World Examples:

- Tesla's ESG Strategy: Prioritizes electric vehicles and clean energy.
- Microsoft's Carbon Neutral Commitment: Aims to be carbon-negative by 2030.
- BlackRock's ESG Investments: Invests in companies with strong sustainability policies.
- Starbucks' Ethical Sourcing: Ensures fair wages and sustainable coffee farming.

How to Implement ESG in Decision-Making:

✓ Encourage businesses to adopt sustainable supply chains.

✓ Support companies with strong ESG policies.

✓ Promote transparency in corporate sustainability reports.

✓ Demand social responsibility from large corporations.

Mindsets that are required for Advanced Sustainability

1. Reflective Mindset (Self-Awareness)
- **Mindset:** Recognize the impact of personal choices on the environment and society.
- **How to Build It:**
    - **Track Your Impact:** Use tools like carbon footprint calculators to understand your environmental impact.
    - **Educate Yourself:** Learn about sustainable practices in daily life (e.g., minimalism, slow fashion).
    - **Reflect:** Regularly assess your habits and make improvements.
- **Behavior:**
    - Reduce waste by avoiding single-use plastics.
    - Choose eco-friendly products and support sustainable brands.
    - Educate others on the importance of self-awareness in sustainability.

2. Resilient Mindset (Crisis Management in Climate Change)
- **Mindset:** Prepare for and respond to climate-related crises with adaptability and foresight.
- **How to Build It:**
    - **Learn from Examples:** Study successful crisis management strategies like the Netherlands' flood management or Bangladesh's cyclone preparedness.
    - **Plan Ahead:** Develop emergency response plans for your community or organization.
    - **Collaborate:** Work with governments, NGOs, and businesses to build resilience.
- **Behavior:**
    - Support disaster risk reduction policies.
    - Invest in climate-resilient infrastructure.
    - Educate communities on climate emergency preparedness.

3. Strategic Mindset (Global Climate Resilience Strategies)

- **Mindset:** Think long-term and strategically to build systems that can withstand climate challenges.
- **How to Build It:**
  - **Study Resilience Models:** Learn from initiatives like Africa's Great Green Wall or Singapore's Green Plan 2030.
  - **Innovate:** Explore new technologies and practices for climate adaptation.
  - **Advocate:** Push for policies that promote renewable energy, water conservation, and green infrastructure.
- **Behavior:**
  - Support reforestation and ecosystem restoration projects.
  - Advocate for climate adaptation policies at local and national levels.
  - Promote community-driven sustainability initiatives.

4. Conservation Mindset (Deforestation)

- **Mindset:** Understand the critical role of forests in biodiversity, climate regulation, and community livelihoods.

- **How to Build It:**
  - **Educate Yourself:** Learn about the causes and impacts of deforestation.
  - **Support Conservation:** Participate in or donate to reforestation programs.
  - **Advocate:** Push for stricter forest conservation policies and sustainable supply chains.
- **Behavior:**
  - Reduce paper and wood consumption.
  - Boycott products linked to illegal deforestation (e.g., unsustainable palm oil).
  - Support reforestation and tree-planting initiatives.

5. Ethical Governance Mindset (Role of ESG in Decision-Making)

- **Mindset:** Integrate environmental, social, and governance (ESG) principles into business and policy decisions.

- **How to Build It:**
  - ○ **Learn ESG Frameworks:** Understand how ESG metrics guide ethical decision-making.
  - ○ **Advocate for Transparency:** Push for corporate sustainability reporting and accountability.
  - ○ **Invest Responsibly:** Support companies with strong ESG policies.

- **Behavior:**
  - ○ Encourage businesses to adopt sustainable supply chains.
  - ○ Support companies with strong ESG policies.
  - ○ Demand transparency in corporate sustainability reports.

Conclusion – The Power of the Grey HAT Certification

The Grey HAT Certification develops advanced sustainability leadership skills in climate resilience, crisis management, and ethical decision-making. It empowers individuals to take action against climate change at personal, corporate, and policy levels.

✓ Self-Awareness builds responsible personal habits.

✓ Crisis Management ensures communities survive climate disasters.

✓ Climate Resilience Strategies help adapt to climate risks.

✓ Deforestation Prevention protects ecosystems and biodiversity.

✓ ESG Decision-Making integrates sustainability into global businesses.

CHAPTER 10

Pink HAT Certification (Advanced - Level 3) - Ethical Leadership, Global Resource Management, Global and Local Sustainability Policies, Social Impact Measurement

The Pink HAT Certification is an advanced-level certification within the ZHA Sustainability Mindset Framework, focusing on ethical leadership, global resource management, sustainability policies, and social impact measurement. This certification is designed for leaders, policymakers, sustainability professionals, and corporate executives who aim to drive ethical governance, responsible resource use, and measurable social impact.

Key Focus Areas:

✓ Ethical Leadership – Leading with integrity and sustainability.
✓ Global Resource Management – Ensuring responsible consumption and fair distribution.

✓ Global & Local Sustainability Policies – Implementing impactful regulations and guidelines.
✓ Social Impact Measurement – Evaluating sustainability initiatives' effectiveness.

1. Ethical Leadership – Leading with Integrity & Responsibility

What is Ethical Leadership in Sustainability?

Ethical leadership is the practice of making decisions that are morally sound, environmentally responsible, and socially fair. It involves corporate transparency, fairness, and sustainable decision-making that benefits both people and the planet.

Benefits of Ethical Leadership:

- Promotes trust and credibility in organizations and governance.
- Encourages sustainable and long-term decision-making.
- Fosters a culture of environmental and social responsibility.
- Reduces corporate greenwashing and unethical practices.

Real-World Examples:

- Patagonia's Environmental Responsibility: The company donates a portion of profits to environmental causes and promotes sustainable fashion.
- Unilever's Ethical Supply Chain: Reduces carbon footprint, supports fair wages, and ensures ethical sourcing.
- Paul Polman (Former CEO of Unilever): Advocated for sustainable business strategies and ESG integration.
- Elon Musk (Tesla & SolarCity): Pushed industries towards electric mobility and renewable energy solutions.

How to Implement Ethical Leadership:

✓ Prioritize sustainability over short-term profits.
✓ Promote transparency in sustainability reporting.
✓ Encourage eco-friendly business models.

✓ Hold corporations and governments accountable for environmental policies.

2. Global Resource Management – Efficient and Equitable Use of Resources

What is Global Resource Management?

Global resource management ensures natural resources like water, energy, and raw materials are used responsibly and fairly across different regions and industries. It prevents overconsumption, reduces waste, and promotes circular economy principles.

Benefits of Responsible Resource Management:

- Prevents depletion of non-renewable resources.
- Ensures fair distribution of resources across nations.
- Reduces waste and promotes sustainable production.
- Encourages innovation in recycling and reuse.

Real-World Examples:

- Singapore's Water Management Strategy: Uses desalination, water recycling, and conservation to ensure a sustainable supply.
- Sweden's Waste-to-Energy Model: Converts 99% of its waste into energy instead of landfilling.
- Coca-Cola's Water Stewardship Program: Aims to replenish all the water it uses in production.
- Circular Economy in the European Union: Policies encourage reuse, repair, and sustainable production.

How to Improve Global Resource Management:

✓ Promote circular economy models.
✓ Reduce dependency on finite natural resources.
✓ Support water conservation and renewable energy adoption.
✓ Advocate for responsible mining, forestry, and agriculture.

3. Global & Local Sustainability Policies – Implementing Systematic Change

What are Sustainability Policies?

Sustainability policies at the global and local levels ensure laws, regulations, and incentives drive sustainable practices in industries, cities, and communities. These policies can include carbon taxes, plastic bans, renewable energy mandates, and conservation laws.

Benefits of Strong Sustainability Policies:

- Reduces environmental damage and resource depletion.
- Encourages corporate responsibility and accountability.
- Provides incentives for sustainable innovation and green jobs.
- Improves public health by reducing pollution and waste.

Real-World Examples:

- Paris Agreement (Global Climate Accord): Nations commit to reducing greenhouse gas emissions.
- India's Plastic Ban: Bans single-use plastics to reduce pollution.
- Costa Rica's Renewable Energy Policy: 99% of electricity comes from renewable sources.
- EU's Green Deal: Aims for carbon neutrality by 2050 through strict sustainability policies.

How to Strengthen Sustainability Policies:

✓ Support local and global climate action agreements.

✓ Push for government accountability in climate policies.

✓ Promote incentives for green industries and sustainable businesses.

✓ Advocate for stricter regulations on pollution and waste management.

4. Social Impact Measurement – Evaluating Sustainability Success

What is Social Impact Measurement?

Social impact measurement is the process of assessing the effectiveness of sustainability initiatives in achieving real-world benefits for communities, economies, and the environment.

Benefits of Measuring Social Impact:

- Ensures sustainability projects meet their goals.
- Helps businesses and governments allocate resources effectively.
- Provides transparency in corporate and nonprofit sustainability programs.
- Encourages data-driven decision-making for sustainable development.

Real-World Examples:

- B Corp Certification: Evaluates companies on their social and environmental impact.
- Impact Investing by BlackRock: Funds companies with measurable social and environmental goals.
- UN Sustainable Development Goals (SDGs) Tracker: Tracks global progress on sustainability targets.
- Social Return on Investment (SROI) Model: Measures financial value of social impact programs.

How to Improve Social Impact Measurement:

✓ Use data-driven sustainability metrics.
✓ Encourage companies to report ESG progress transparently.
✓ Develop standardized frameworks for impact assessment.
✓ Ensure sustainability projects align with real-world needs.

Mindsets that are required for this Advanced Sustainability Certification:

1. Ethical Leadership Mindset

- **Mindset:** Lead with integrity, prioritizing long-term environmental and social responsibility over short-term gains.
- **How to Build It:**
  - **Educate Yourself:** Study ethical leadership models like Patagonia's environmental responsibility or Unilever's sustainable supply chain.
  - **Practice Transparency:** Be open about your organization's sustainability efforts and challenges.
  - **Advocate for Accountability:** Push for corporate and governmental transparency in sustainability reporting.
- **Behavior:**
  - Prioritize sustainability in decision-making.
  - Promote eco-friendly business models.
  - Hold organizations accountable for their environmental and social impact.

2. Resource Stewardship Mindset (Global Resource Management)

- **Mindset:** Recognize the finite nature of resources and the need for equitable distribution.
- **How to Build It:**
  - **Learn Best Practices:** Study examples like Singapore's water management or Sweden's waste-to-energy model.
  - **Innovate:** Explore circular economy principles and sustainable production methods.
  - **Advocate:** Push for policies that promote responsible resource use.
- **Behavior:**
  - Support circular economy initiatives.
  - Reduce dependency on non-renewable resources.
  - Advocate for water conservation and renewable energy adoption.

3. Policy Advocacy Mindset (Global & Local Sustainability Policies)

- **Mindset:** Understand the power of policies to drive systemic change and ensure accountability.
- **How to Build It:**
  - **Study Policy Frameworks:** Learn about global agreements like the Paris Agreement and local initiatives like India's plastic ban.
  - **Engage with Policymakers:** Advocate for stronger sustainability regulations and incentives.
  - **Collaborate:** Work with governments, NGOs, and businesses to implement impactful policies.

- **Behavior:**
  - Support climate action agreements and renewable energy mandates.
  - Push for stricter regulations on pollution and waste management.
  - Promote incentives for green industries and sustainable businesses.

4. Impact-Driven Mindset (Social Impact Measurement)

- **Mindset:** Focus on measurable outcomes to ensure sustainability initiatives deliver real-world benefits.
- **How to Build It:**
  - **Learn Metrics:** Understand frameworks like B Corp Certification, SDG Trackers, and Social Return on Investment (SROI).
  - **Track Progress:** Use data-driven tools to measure the effectiveness of sustainability projects.
  - **Advocate for Transparency:** Push for standardized reporting and accountability in sustainability efforts.
- **Behavior:**
  - Use sustainability metrics to guide decision-making.
  - Encourage transparent ESG reporting.
  - Align projects with real-world needs and measurable goals.

Conclusion – The Power of the Pink HAT Certification

The Pink HAT Certification develops ethical leadership, responsible resource management, policy advocacy, and social impact assessment skills. It equips individuals with advanced tools to lead sustainability-driven organizations, governments, and initiatives.

✓ Ethical Leadership ensures decision-making aligns with environmental and social responsibility.
✓ Global Resource Management promotes sustainable consumption and fair resource distribution.
✓ Sustainability Policies drive systemic change at local and global levels.
✓ Social Impact Measurement ensures that sustainability efforts are effective and transparent.

CHAPTER 11

Black HAT Certification (Expert - Level 4) - Advanced ESG Compliance Strategies, Carbon Emission Projects, Precision Farming, AI-powered conservationl, Blockchain for Carbon Credits & Smart Grid Technologies

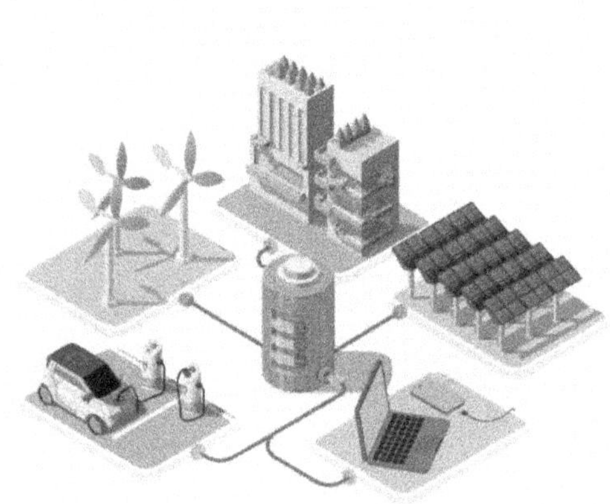

The Black HAT Certification represents the highest level of expertise within the ZHA Sustainability Mindset Practitioner's Framework. It focuses on cutting-edge sustainability technologies, advanced Environmental, Social, and Governance (ESG) compliance strategies, and innovative solutions for carbon reduction, conservation, and resource management.

This certification is tailored for corporate leaders, sustainability strategists, policymakers, technology innovators, and environmental professionals who drive large-scale sustainability transformation.

Key Focus Areas:

✓ **Advanced ESG Compliance Strategies** – Ensuring businesses align with international sustainability regulations.
✓ **Carbon Emission Projects** – Developing initiatives to offset and reduce carbon footprints.
✓ **Precision Farming** – Using technology to optimize agricultural efficiency and sustainability.
✓ **AI-powered Conservation** – Applying artificial intelligence to monitor and protect ecosystems.
✓ **Blockchain for Carbon Credits** – Enhancing transparency and accountability in carbon offset markets.
✓ **Smart Grid Technologies** – Revolutionizing energy management through intelligent systems.

1. Advanced ESG Compliance Strategies – Driving Corporate Sustainability & Accountability

What is ESG Compliance?

Environmental, Social, and Governance (ESG) compliance ensures that **businesses adhere to sustainability, ethical governance, and social responsibility standards**. Companies are increasingly required to meet **global ESG regulations** to attract investors, avoid penalties, and maintain their corporate reputation.

Benefits of ESG Compliance:

- Reduces environmental risks and ensures corporate responsibility.
- Attracts ESG-focused investors and stakeholders.
- Enhances brand reputation and consumer trust.
- Ensures regulatory compliance, reducing legal and financial risks.

Real-World Examples:

- **Tesla's ESG Leadership:** Focuses on sustainable energy, supply chain transparency, and ethical governance.
- **Microsoft's Carbon Negative Pledge:** Aims to remove all historical carbon emissions by 2050.
- **European Union's ESG Reporting Regulations:** Requires companies to disclose sustainability risks and carbon footprints.
- **Global ESG Indexes (MSCI, FTSE4Good):** Ranks companies based on sustainability and governance performance.

How to Strengthen ESG Compliance:

✓ **Integrate ESG metrics** into business decision-making.

✓ **Adopt sustainable supply chains** to reduce carbon impact.

✓ **Ensure transparent ESG reporting** to investors and stakeholders.

✓ **Implement ethical labor practices** to improve social responsibility.

2. Carbon Emission Projects – Reducing and Offsetting Global Carbon Footprints

What are Carbon Emission Projects?

Carbon emission projects focus on **reducing greenhouse gas emissions, capturing carbon from the atmosphere, and investing in carbon offset programs** such as reforestation, renewable energy, and carbon capture technology.

Benefits of Carbon Emission Projects:

- **Helps industries meet net-zero carbon goals.**
- **Encourages investment in clean energy and reforestation.**
- **Offsets unavoidable carbon emissions through verified carbon credits.**
- **Enhances corporate social responsibility and ESG compliance.**

Real-World Examples:

- **Amazon's Climate Pledge Fund:** Invests in carbon reduction technologies.
- **Google's Renewable Energy Commitment:** Runs all data centers on carbon-free energy.
- **India's Carbon Credit Trading System:** Encourages industries to reduce emissions and trade carbon credits.
- **Direct Air Capture (DAC) by Climeworks:** Removes CO_2 directly from the atmosphere for long-term storage.

How to Implement Carbon Emission Strategies:

✓ **Adopt energy-efficient technologies** to cut carbon footprints.

✓ **Invest in carbon offset projects** like reforestation and renewable energy.

✓ **Utilize carbon capture and storage (CCS) technologies**.

✓ **Encourage corporate carbon neutrality** through verified carbon credit programs.

3. Precision Farming – Sustainable Agriculture through Smart Technology

What is Precision Farming?

Precision farming is the use of **technology-driven approaches in agriculture** to **optimize crop yields, reduce resource waste, and minimize environmental impact**. It integrates **AI, IoT, drones, and soil monitoring** to ensure sustainable and efficient farming.

Benefits of Precision Farming:

- Reduces water, fertilizer, and pesticide use.
- Increases crop productivity while reducing environmental damage.
- Improves soil health and conserves biodiversity.
- Enhances resilience to climate change through data-driven farming.

Real-World Examples:

- **John Deere's Smart Tractors:** Uses AI to optimize seeding and irrigation.
- **AgriTech Startups (CropX, Indigo Ag):** AI-based soil and climate monitoring.
- **Vertical Farming by AeroFarms:** Reduces water usage by 95% while growing crops indoors.
- **Precision Irrigation by Netafim:** Drip irrigation system minimizing water waste.

How to Implement Precision Farming:

✓ Use **IoT sensors for real-time soil monitoring**.

✓ Apply **AI and drones to analyze crop health**.

✓ Reduce **chemical use through targeted application**.

✓ Promote **regenerative agricultural practices**.

4. AI-powered Conservation – Using Artificial Intelligence to Protect Ecosystems

What is AI-powered Conservation?

AI-powered conservation applies **machine learning, big data, and AI-powered sensors** to **monitor, predict, and protect endangered species and natural habitats.**

✓ **Benefits of AI-powered Conservation:**

- Identifies threats to biodiversity in real-time.
- Improves accuracy in wildlife population tracking.
- Detects illegal deforestation and poaching activities.
- Enhances conservation efforts with automated surveillance.

Real-World Examples:

- **Google AI for Wildlife Tracking:** Uses image recognition to monitor endangered species.
- **IBM's AI-driven Forest Monitoring:** Detects deforestation risks through satellite imaging.
- **DeepMind's AI Climate Models:** Predicts the impact of climate change on ecosystems.
- **The Ocean Cleanup's AI-powered System:** Removes plastic waste from oceans using machine learning.

How to Implement AI-powered Conservation:

✓ Use **AI image recognition** for wildlife tracking.
✓ Apply **satellite monitoring to detect deforestation**.
✓ Develop **AI-driven climate models** for proactive conservation.
✓ Implement **smart surveillance for anti-poaching**.

5. Blockchain for Carbon Credits – Enhancing Transparency in Sustainability Markets

What is Blockchain for Carbon Credits?

Blockchain technology is used to **track, verify, and trade carbon credits in a transparent and decentralized system**, ensuring that **carbon offset programs are legitimate and effective**.

Benefits of Blockchain in Carbon Trading:

- Prevents fraudulent carbon offset claims.
- Improves transparency in carbon credit transactions.
- Encourages corporate accountability in emissions reduction.

- Simplifies carbon trading across global markets.

Real-World Examples:

- **IBM & Energy Blockchain Lab:** Developed a blockchain-based carbon trading platform.
- **KlimaDAO:** Uses blockchain for transparent carbon credit purchases.
- **Toucan Protocol:** Connects carbon credits with decentralized finance (DeFi).

How to Leverage Blockchain for Sustainability:

✓ Implement **secure, trackable carbon credit registries**.

✓ Use **blockchain-based contracts for verified carbon offset projects**.

✓ Develop **carbon trading platforms with transparent transactions**.

Mindsets that are required for this Expert Sustainability Certification:

1. Strategic Compliance Mindset (Advanced ESG Compliance Strategies)
- **Mindset:** Understand that ESG compliance is not just a regulatory requirement but a strategic advantage for long-term sustainability.
- **How to Build It:**
    - **Educate Yourself:** Study global ESG frameworks like the EU's ESG Reporting Regulations or MSCI ESG Indexes.
    - **Integrate ESG Metrics:** Align business strategies with sustainability goals.
    - **Advocate for Transparency:** Push for clear and honest ESG reporting.
- **Behavior:**
    - Adopt sustainable supply chains and ethical labor practices.
    - Ensure transparent ESG reporting to stakeholders.
    - Align corporate strategies with international sustainability standards.

2. Carbon Neutrality Mindset (Carbon Emission Projects)
- **Mindset:** Commit to reducing and offsetting carbon emissions to achieve net-zero goals.

* **How to Build It:**
  * **Learn Best Practices:** Study initiatives like Amazon's Climate Pledge Fund or Google's renewable energy commitments.
  * **Innovate:** Explore carbon capture technologies and renewable energy solutions.
  * **Collaborate:** Work with industries and governments to scale carbon reduction projects.
* **Behavior:**
  * Invest in carbon offset projects like reforestation and renewable energy.
  * Implement energy-efficient technologies to reduce emissions.
  * Advocate for corporate carbon neutrality through verified carbon credits.

3. Tech-Driven Agriculture Mindset (Precision Farming)

* **Mindset:** Embrace technology to optimize agricultural efficiency and sustainability.
* **How to Build It:**
  * **Learn About Precision Tools:** Study technologies like IoT sensors, AI, and drones used in farming.
  * **Experiment:** Implement precision farming techniques in small-scale projects.
  * **Advocate:** Promote regenerative agriculture and sustainable farming practices.
* **Behavior:**
  * Use IoT sensors for real-time soil and crop monitoring.
  * Apply AI and drones to analyze crop health and optimize yields.
  * Reduce chemical use through targeted and data-driven farming.

4. AI-Powered Conservation Mindset (AI-powered Conservation)

* **Mindset:** Leverage artificial intelligence to protect ecosystems and biodiversity.
* **How to Build It:**
  * **Study AI Applications:** Learn how AI is used in wildlife tracking, deforestation detection, and climate modeling.

- ○ **Collaborate:** Partner with tech companies and conservation organizations to implement AI solutions.
  - ○ **Innovate:** Develop AI-driven tools for real-time ecosystem monitoring.
- **Behavior:**
  - ○ Use AI image recognition for wildlife population tracking.
  - ○ Apply satellite monitoring to detect illegal deforestation.
  - ○ Implement AI-powered surveillance to combat poaching.

5. Blockchain Transparency Mindset (Blockchain for Carbon Credits)

- **Mindset:** Use blockchain technology to ensure transparency and accountability in carbon credit markets.
- **How to Build It:**
  - ○ **Learn Blockchain Basics:** Understand how blockchain works and its applications in sustainability.
  - ○ **Experiment:** Pilot blockchain-based carbon credit tracking systems.
  - ○ **Advocate:** Push for decentralized and transparent carbon trading platforms.
- **Behavior:**
  - ○ Implement blockchain-based carbon credit registries.
  - ○ Use smart contracts for verified carbon offset projects.
  - ○ Develop transparent carbon trading platforms.

Conclusion – The Power of the Black HAT Certification

The **Black HAT Certification** prepares sustainability professionals to implement **advanced ESG strategies, technology-driven conservation, carbon reduction initiatives, and blockchain-based sustainability solutions**.

✓ **Advanced ESG Compliance** improves corporate sustainability accountability.

✓ **Carbon Emission Projects** drive large-scale climate action.

✓ **Precision Farming** ensures sustainable agricultural practices.

✓ **AI-powered Conservation** protects biodiversity with intelligent solutions.

✓ **Blockchain for Carbon Credits** enables transparent carbon offset trading.

CHAPTER 12

Gold HAT Certification (Expert - Level 4) - Behavioral Economics & Consumer Behavior, Sustainability in International Trade, sustainable supply chain management, sustainability reporting, Advanced Climate Adaptation Solutions

The Gold HAT Certification is designed for business leaders, policymakers, sustainability strategists, and economic experts who aim to integrate sustainability into global markets, supply chains, corporate governance, and climate adaptation strategies.

This certification covers sustainability in international trade, sustainable supply chain management, behavioral economics, consumer behavior, and advanced sustainability reporting using global frameworks like GRI, SASB, and TCFD. It also includes cutting-edge climate adaptation strategies to address global environmental challenges.

Key Focus Areas:

✓ Behavioral Economics & Consumer Behavior – Understanding how sustainability influences consumer decisions.

✓ Sustainability in International Trade – Integrating sustainable practices in global commerce.

✓ Sustainable Supply Chain Management – Ensuring ethical, low-carbon, and resilient supply chains.

✓ Sustainability Reporting – Mastering GRI, SASB, and TCFD frameworks for corporate transparency.

✓ Advanced Climate Adaptation Strategies – Developing solutions to mitigate climate change risks.

1. Behavioral Economics & Consumer Behavior – Driving Green Consumer Choices

What is Behavioral Economics in Sustainability?

Behavioral economics studies how people make economic decisions based on psychology, emotions, and social influences. In sustainability, it examines how consumers adopt eco-friendly habits, choose sustainable products, and support green businesses.

Benefits of Understanding Consumer Behavior in Sustainability:

- Encourages businesses to design sustainable products that appeal to eco-conscious consumers.
- Helps policymakers create effective incentives for sustainability adoption.

- Influences consumer purchasing decisions towards ethical brands.
- Reduces environmental impact by shifting demand toward greener alternatives.

Real-World Examples:

- IKEA's Circular Business Model: Offers buy-back programs to encourage furniture reuse.
- Unilever's Sustainable Living Brands: Products with sustainability benefits grow 69% faster than others.
- Carbon Labeling by Oatly & Quorn: Shows carbon footprint on packaging to influence consumer choices.
- Government Plastic Bag Bans: Encourages consumers to adopt reusable alternatives.

How to Apply Behavioral Economics to Sustainability:

✓ Use "nudge theory" – Encourage green behavior through incentives and easy choices.

✓ Apply carbon labeling – Help consumers make informed decisions.

✓ Create sustainable loyalty programs – Reward eco-friendly behavior.

✓ Promote ethical storytelling – Influence buying decisions through sustainability narratives.

2. Sustainability in International Trade – Green Global Commerce

What is Sustainable Trade?

Sustainable international trade integrates environmental, social, and ethical practices into global trade policies. It ensures that goods and services are produced with minimal environmental harm and fair labor conditions.

Benefits of Sustainability in Trade:

- Reduces carbon emissions from global supply chains.
- Encourages fair trade and ethical labor practices.
- Protects biodiversity and prevents over-exploitation of natural resources.
- Drives global cooperation for sustainable economic growth.

Real-World Examples:

- European Green Deal & Carbon Border Adjustment Mechanism (CBAM): Applies carbon tariffs on imports based on emissions.
- Fair Trade Certification: Ensures ethical sourcing of coffee, cocoa, and textiles.
- China's Green Belt & Road Initiative: Focuses on eco-friendly infrastructure development.
- Amazon's Climate Pledge Friendly Label: Promotes sustainable international products.

How to Promote Sustainability in Trade:

✓ Adopt fair trade certification for ethically sourced products.

✓ Implement carbon pricing to reduce emissions in global supply chains.

✓ Support trade agreements that prioritize environmental and social standards.

✓ Encourage transparency in sourcing and production.

3. Sustainable Supply Chain Management – Ethical & Resilient Global Logistics

What is Sustainable Supply Chain Management?

Sustainable supply chain management (SSCM) optimizes logistics, manufacturing, and distribution to reduce environmental and social impacts. It involves ethical sourcing, carbon reduction, and circular economy practices.

Benefits of a Sustainable Supply Chain:

- Reduces carbon footprint from transportation and manufacturing.
- Enhances brand reputation and customer loyalty.
- Minimizes waste through circular economy principles.
- Improves operational efficiency and cost savings.

Real-World Examples:

- Walmart's Project Gigaton: Aims to reduce 1 billion metric tons of greenhouse gases from supply chains.

- Apple's Carbon-Neutral Supply Chain Plan: Targets 100% clean energy for suppliers.
- Patagonia's Fair Trade Program: Ensures ethical manufacturing and living wages.
- Coca-Cola's "World Without Waste" Initiative: Focuses on 100% recyclable packaging.

How to Implement Sustainable Supply Chains:

✓ Reduce emissions through energy-efficient logistics.

✓ Adopt ethical labor standards for fair wages and working conditions.

✓ Minimize packaging waste with biodegradable materials.

✓ Invest in renewable energy for manufacturing.

4. Sustainability Reporting – Mastering GRI, SASB, and TCFD Frameworks

What is Sustainability Reporting?

Sustainability reporting measures and discloses a company's environmental, social, and governance (ESG) performance. Leading frameworks include:

GRI (Global Reporting Initiative): Standardizes corporate sustainability disclosure.
SASB (Sustainability Accounting Standards Board): Focuses on financially material ESG issues.

TCFD (Task Force on Climate-Related Financial Disclosures): Guides companies on climate risk reporting.

Benefits of Sustainability Reporting:

- Enhances corporate transparency and investor confidence.
- Helps businesses manage risks related to climate change.
- Attracts ESG-focused investments.
- Ensures regulatory compliance and stakeholder trust.

Real-World Examples:

- Tesla's ESG Reports: Discloses battery recycling and supply chain sustainability.
- BlackRock's Sustainability Investment Strategy: Uses TCFD to guide ESG investments.
- Nike's GRI Report: Highlights progress on reducing emissions and waste.

How to Improve Sustainability Reporting:

✓ Align disclosures with global ESG frameworks.

✓ Use data analytics to track sustainability performance.

✓ Engage stakeholders to build trust and transparency.

✓ Integrate climate risk assessment into corporate decision-making.

5. Advanced Climate Adaptation Strategies – Resilient Solutions for a Changing World

What is Climate Adaptation?

Climate adaptation involves proactive strategies to mitigate the risks of climate change by strengthening resilience in communities, businesses, and ecosystems.

Benefits of Climate Adaptation Strategies:

- Protects communities from extreme weather events.
- Strengthens infrastructure to withstand climate risks.
- Safeguards food security and water resources.

- Reduces economic losses due to climate-related disasters.

Real-World Examples:

- Netherlands' Flood Resilience Plan: Uses floating homes and water barriers.
- California's Wildfire Adaptation Strategy: Implements early warning systems and fire-resistant infrastructure.
- African Union's Climate Resilience Projects: Enhances drought-resistant agriculture.

How to Develop Climate Adaptation Strategies:

✓ Invest in resilient infrastructure to withstand extreme weather.

✓ Implement nature-based solutions like reforestation.

✓ Improve early warning systems for climate-related disasters.

✓ Strengthen local and global cooperation on climate action.

Mindsets that are required for Expert-Level Sustainability Certification:

1. Behavioral Insight Mindset (Behavioral Economics & Consumer Behavior)

- **Mindset:** Understand how psychology and social influences drive consumer decisions and use this knowledge to promote sustainable choices.
- **How to Build It:**
    - **Study Behavioral Economics:** Learn about concepts like nudge theory and carbon labeling.
    - **Experiment:** Test incentives and messaging to encourage eco-friendly behavior.
    - **Advocate:** Promote policies that make sustainable choices easier for consumers.
- **Behavior:**
    - Use carbon labeling to inform consumer decisions.
    - Create loyalty programs that reward sustainable behavior.

- Design marketing campaigns that highlight ethical and environmental benefits.

2. Global Trade Mindset (Sustainability in International Trade)

- **Mindset:** Recognize the interconnectedness of global trade and its impact on sustainability.
- **How to Build It:**
  - **Learn Best Practices:** Study initiatives like the European Green Deal or Fair Trade Certification.
  - **Collaborate:** Work with governments and businesses to promote sustainable trade policies.
  - **Advocate:** Push for carbon pricing and ethical sourcing in global supply chains.
- **Behavior:**
  - Support fair trade and ethical sourcing practices.
  - Advocate for carbon tariffs on high-emission imports.
  - Promote transparency in global trade practices.

3. Ethical Supply Chain Mindset (Sustainable Supply Chain Management)

- **Mindset:** Commit to reducing the environmental and social impact of supply chains.
- **How to Build It:**
  - **Study SSCM Models:** Learn from companies like Walmart and Apple that have implemented sustainable supply chains.
  - **Innovate:** Explore circular economy principles and renewable energy solutions.
  - **Collaborate:** Partner with suppliers to reduce emissions and waste.
- **Behavior:**
  - Adopt energy-efficient logistics and manufacturing processes.
  - Ensure fair wages and ethical labor practices.
  - Minimize packaging waste and use biodegradable materials.

4. Transparency Mindset (Sustainability Reporting)

- **Mindset:** Embrace transparency and accountability in corporate sustainability efforts.
- **How to Build It:**
  - **Learn Reporting Frameworks:** Study GRI, SASB, and TCFD standards.
  - **Integrate ESG Metrics:** Align business strategies with sustainability goals.
  - **Advocate:** Push for standardized and transparent ESG reporting.
- **Behavior:**
  - Align sustainability reports with global frameworks like GRI and TCFD.
  - Use data analytics to track and improve sustainability performance.
  - Engage stakeholders to build trust and transparency.

5. Resilience Mindset (Advanced Climate Adaptation Strategies)

- **Mindset:** Prepare for and adapt to the impacts of climate change through proactive strategies.
- **How to Build It:**
  - **Study Adaptation Models:** Learn from examples like the Netherlands' flood resilience plan or California's wildfire strategy.
  - **Innovate:** Explore nature-based solutions and resilient infrastructure.
  - **Collaborate:** Work with communities and governments to implement adaptation measures.
- **Behavior:**
  - Invest in resilient infrastructure to withstand extreme weather.
  - Implement early warning systems for climate-related disasters.
  - Promote reforestation and other nature-based solutions.

How to Build These Mindsets

1. **Education:** Learn about sustainability principles, behavioral economics, and global frameworks.
2. **Practice:** Start small—implement sustainable practices in your organization or community.
3. **Collaboration:** Work with others to amplify your impact.
4. **Reflection:** Regularly assess your actions and their alignment with sustainability goals.
5. **Advocacy:** Share your knowledge and inspire others to adopt sustainable practices.

Behaviors for Expert-Level Sustainability

Behavioral Economics & Consumer Behavior

- Use nudge theory: Encourage sustainable choices through incentives and easy options.
- Apply carbon labeling: Help consumers make informed decisions about their carbon footprint.
- Promote ethical storytelling: Highlight the sustainability benefits of products and brands.

Sustainability in International Trade

- Support fair trade: Advocate for ethically sourced products and fair labor practices.
- Implement carbon pricing: Push for carbon tariffs on high-emission imports.
- Promote transparency: Ensure clear and honest reporting of sourcing and production practices

Sustainable Supply Chain Management

- Reduce emissions: Use energy-efficient logistics and renewable energy in manufacturing.
- Adopt ethical labor standards: Ensure fair wages and safe working conditions.

- Minimize waste: Use biodegradable materials and circular economy principles.

Sustainability Reporting

- Align with global frameworks: Use GRI, SASB, and TCFD standards for ESG reporting.
- Track performance: Use data analytics to measure and improve sustainability efforts.
- Engage stakeholders: Build trust through transparent and honest reporting.

Advanced Climate Adaptation Strategies

- Invest in resilient infrastructure: Build systems that can withstand extreme weather.
- Implement early warning systems: Prepare communities for climate-related disasters.
- Promote nature-based solutions: Support reforestation and other ecological strategies.

Conclusion – The Power of the Gold HAT Certification

The Gold HAT Certification equips professionals with expertise in economic sustainability, corporate responsibility, and climate resilience strategies.

✓ Master sustainability reporting for ESG compliance.

✓ Build sustainable global supply chains.

✓ Lead international trade policies toward green transformation.

✓ Apply behavioral economics to shift consumer habits.

✓ Develop climate adaptation solutions for long-term resilience.

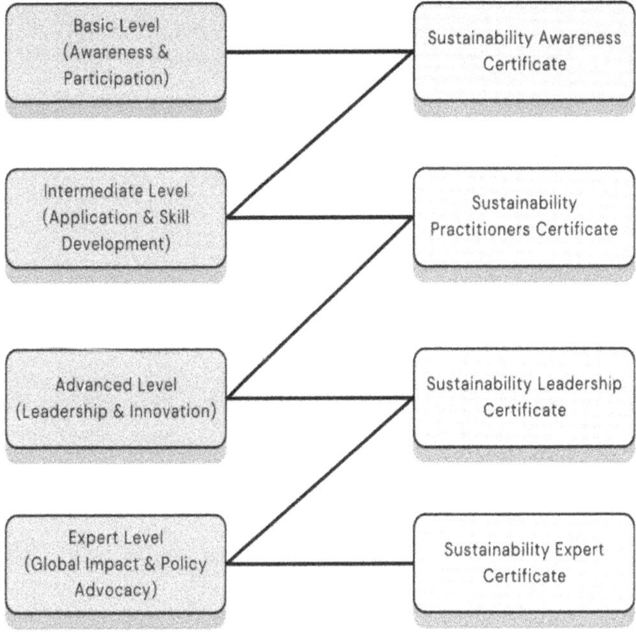

Sustainability leadership at the expert level requires strategic thinking, global collaboration, and innovative problem-solving. The Gold HAT Certification emphasizes the importance of developing mindsets that drive systemic change in consumer behavior, international trade, supply chains, corporate transparency, and climate resilience. These mindsets shape how we approach sustainability challenges and create long-term solutions. Let's explore the mindsets required, how to build them, and the behaviors that align with these principles.

Student Notes:

Student Notes:

Student Notes: